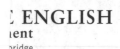

D1454371

Cambridge English

OFFICIAL

FIRST 2

WITH ANSWERS

WITHDRAWN

AUTHENTIC EXAMINATION PAPERS

15 JAN 2019

RECEIVED

CARDIFF AND VALE COLLEGE

Cambridge University Press
www.cambridge.org/elt

Cambridge English Language Assessment
www.cambridgeenglish.org

Information on this title: www.cambridge.org/9781316503577

© Cambridge University Press and UCLES 2016

It is normally necessary for written permission for copying to be obtained
in advance from a publisher. The sample answer sheets at the back of this
book are designed to be copied and distributed in class.
The normal requirements are waived here and it is not necessary to write to
Cambridge University Press for permission for an individual teacher to make copies
for use within his or her own classroom. Only those pages that carry the wording
'© UCLES 2016 Photocopiable' may be copied.

First published 2016

Printed in Spain by GraphyCems

A catalogue record for this publication is available from the British Library

ISBN 978-1-316-50357-7 Student's Book with answers
ISBN 978-1-316-50356-0 Student's Book with answers with Audio
ISBN 978-1-316-50298-3 Student's Book without answers
ISBN 978-1-316-50354-6 Audio CDs (2)

The publishers have no responsibility for the persistence or accuracy
of URLs for external or third-party internet websites referred to in this publication,
and do not guarantee that any content on such websites is, or will remain,
accurate or appropriate. Information regarding prices, travel timetables, and other
factual information given in this work is correct at the time of first printing but
the publishers do not guarantee the accuracy of such information thereafter.

Contents

Introduction

This collection of four complete practice tests comprises papers from the *Cambridge English: First (FCE)* examination; students can practise these tests on their own or with the help of a teacher.

The *Cambridge English: First* examination is part of a suite of general English examinations produced by Cambridge English Language Assessment. This suite consists of five examinations that have similar characteristics but are designed for different levels of English language ability. Within the five levels, *Cambridge English: First* is at Level B2 in the Council of Europe's *Common European Framework of Reference for Languages: Learning, teaching, assessment*. It has also been accredited by Ofqual, the statutory regulatory authority in England, at Level 1 in the National Qualifications Framework. The *Cambridge English: First* examination is widely recognised in commerce and industry, and in individual university faculties and other educational institutions.

Examination	Council of Europe Framework Level	UK National Qualifications Framework Level
Cambridge English: Proficiency *Certificate of Proficiency in English (CPE)*	C2	3
Cambridge English: Advanced *Certificate in Advanced English (CAE)*	C1	2
Cambridge English: First *First Certificate in English (FCE)*	B2	1
Cambridge English: Preliminary *Preliminary English Test (PET)*	B1	Entry 3
Cambridge English: Key *Key English Test (KET)*	A2	Entry 2

Further information

The information contained in this practice book is designed to be an overview of the exam. For a full description of all of the above exams, including information about task types, testing focus and preparation, please see the relevant handbooks which can be obtained from Cambridge English Language Assessment at the address below or from the website at: www.CambridgeEnglish.org

Cambridge English Language Assessment
1 Hills Road
Cambridge CB1 2EU
United Kingdom

Telephone: +44 1223 553997
Fax: +44 1223 553621
email: helpdesk@cambridgeenglish.org

The structure of *Cambridge English: First* – an overview

The *Cambridge English: First* examination consists of four papers.

Reading and Use of English   1 hour 15 minutes
This paper consists of **seven parts**, with 52 questions. For Parts 1 to 4, the test contains texts with accompanying grammar and vocabulary tasks, and separate items with a grammar and vocabulary focus. For Parts 5 to 7, the test contains a range of texts and accompanying reading comprehension tasks.

Writing   1 hour 20 minutes
This paper consists of **two parts** which carry equal marks. In Part 1, which is **compulsory**, candidates have to write an essay of between 140 and 190 words, giving their opinion in response to a task. In Part 2, there are three tasks from which candidates choose **one** to write about. The range of tasks from which questions may be drawn includes an article, an email/letter, a report and a review. In this part, candidates have to write between 140 and 190 words.

Listening   40 minutes (approximately)
This paper consists of **four parts**. Each part contains a recorded text or texts and some questions, including multiple-choice, sentence completion and multiple-matching questions. Each text is heard twice. There is a total of **30 questions**.

Speaking   14 minutes
This paper consists of **four parts**. The standard test format is two candidates and two examiners. One examiner takes part in the conversation while the other examiner listens. Both examiners give marks. Candidates will be given photographs and other visual and written material to look at and talk about. Sometimes candidates will talk with the other candidate, sometimes with the examiner, and sometimes with both.

Grading

Candidates will receive a score on the Cambridge English Scale for each of the four skills and Use of English. The average of these five scores gives the candidate's overall Cambridge English Scale score for the exam. This determines what grade and CEFR level they achieve. All candidates receive a Statement of Results and candidates who pass the examination with Grade A, B or C also receive the *First Certificate in English*. Candidates who achieve Grade A receive the *First Certificate in English* stating that they demonstrated ability at Level C1. Candidates who achieve Grade B or C receive the *First Certificate in English* certificate stating that they demonstrated ability at Level B2. Candidates whose performance is below B2 level, but falls within Level B1, receive a *Cambridge English* certificate stating that they have demonstrated ability at Level B1. Candidates whose performance falls below Level B1 do not receive a certificate.

   For further information on grading and results, go to the website (see page 4).

Test 5

READING AND USE OF ENGLISH (1 hour 15 minutes)

Part 1

For questions **1–8**, read the text below and decide which answer (**A**, **B**, **C** or **D**) best fits each gap. There is an example at the beginning (**0**).

Mark your answers **on the separate answer sheet**.

Example:

0 **A** closed   **B** contained   **C** surrounded   **D** shut

0	A	B	C	D
	⸺	⸺	▬	⸺

Lighting a town

The Norwegian town of Rjukan lies along the floor of a narrow valley, **(0)** .... by sheer mountains. Because of its location, the town, with its 3,400 **(1)** ...., has in the past lived in shadow for half the year. During the day, from late September to mid-March, the town gets no direct natural sunlight at all. Its residents all agreed this **(2)** .... that the town was incredibly depressing during the winter months.

However, that all changed in 2013 with the **(3)** .... of a system of mirrors whose design Martin Anderson, an artist, had first **(4)** .... up with some 12 years earlier. With financial **(5)** .... from the local government and from several prominent business people, Anderson's idea became a **(6)** .... Today, high on the mountain opposite the town, **(7)** .... three large solar-powered, computer-controlled mirrors **(8)** .... the precise movement of the sun across the winter sky, reflecting its rays onto the town's market square and flooding it in bright sunlight.

1	**A** totals	**B** populations	**C** numbers	**D** inhabitants
2	**A** meant	**B** explained	**C** showed	**D** made
3	**A** ending	**B** conclusion	**C** completion	**D** result
4	**A** brought	**B** come	**C** caught	**D** got
5	**A** budget	**B** cost	**C** expense	**D** investment
6	**A** reality	**B** truth	**C** principle	**D** practicality
7	**A** find	**B** sit	**C** stay	**D** hold
8	**A** passing	**B** following	**C** proceeding	**D** continuing

Part 2

For questions **9–16**, read the text below and think of the word which best fits each gap. Use only **one** word in each gap. There is an example at the beginning (**0**).

Write your answers **IN CAPITAL LETTERS on the separate answer sheet.**

Example: | 0 | | T | O | | | | | | | | | | | | | | | | |

The homing instinct

The homing instinct is what makes certain animals, birds and fish return (**0**) .... the place they consider home. Cats often have this instinct. It was particularly strong in an American cat called Ninja, which disappeared shortly (**9**) .... its owners had taken it to their new home; a year later the cat turned up at its old home even (**10**) .... this was 1,360 kilometres away from (**11**) .... its owners were now living. Other cats may not travel so far but many (**12**) .... on going back to their old home. Pilsbury, an English cat, made a 13-kilometre journey back to its former home 40 times in spite of having to cross several busy roads to (**13**) .... so.

Pigeons also have the homing instinct and, ever (**14**) .... ancient times, human beings have used them to carry messages back home. However, cat owners, (**15**) .... have to keep returning to their old address in (**16**) .... to bring their cat home, tend to find the homing instinct simply irritating rather than useful or interesting!

Part 3

For questions **17–24**, read the text below. Use the word given in capitals at the end of some of the lines to form a word that fits in the gap **in the same line**. There is an example at the beginning (**0**).

Write your answers **IN CAPITAL LETTERS on the separate answer sheet**.

Example:

| 0 | F | A | N | T | A | S | T | I | C | | | | | | | | |

The oldest house in Britain

It was warm, round, had a **(0)** .... view of a lake and appears to   **FANTASY**

have been occupied for several hundred years. Welcome to the

oldest house in the UK, which was found with other fascinating

relics **(17)** .... at a site in North Yorkshire. These remains are   **NEAR**

transforming our **(18)** .... of how Britain's earliest inhabitants lived.   **KNOW**

The structure was 3.5 metres in **(19)** .... and was supported by a   **WIDE**

circle of wooden posts. Dark, decayed matter at the centre of the ruin

suggests the possibility of a roof entirely made of grasses. **(20)** ....   **INVESTIGATE**

of the remains by scientists revealed that the building stood in

8,500 BC. It was **(21)** .... thought that people living in Britain at   **ORIGIN**

this time were nomadic with no fixed homes. But the **(22)** .... of   **DISCOVER**

the oldest known house provides clear **(23)** .... that some of these   **EVIDENT**

people built large permanent structures. Researchers of the site,

however, are **(24)** .... about how long the house will remain the   **SURE**

'oldest' in the UK, because new finds are being made all the time.

Part 4

For questions **25–30**, complete the second sentence so that it has a similar meaning to the first sentence, using the word given. **Do not change the word given.** You must use between **two** and **five** words, including the word given. Here is an example (**0**).

Example:

0 A very friendly taxi driver drove us into town.

DRIVEN

We ………………………………………… a very friendly taxi driver.

The gap can be filled by the words 'were driven into town by', so you write:

Example:	0	*WERE DRIVEN INTO TOWN BY*

Write **only** the missing words **IN CAPITAL LETTERS on the separate answer sheet.**

---

25 I haven't decided what sort of job I'd like to do when I leave college.

MIND

I haven't made ………………………………………… the sort of job I'd like to do when I leave college.

26 Tony never took any notice of the advice people gave him.

ATTENTION

Tony never ………………………………………… the advice people gave him.

27 Mary didn't ring us last night because she knew we were going out.

WOULD

Mary ………………………………………… us last night if she hadn't known we were going out.

28 I am planning to go to the football match, unless they cancel it because of the weather.

DUE

If the football match .... the weather, I am planning to go to it.

29 Louise didn't really feel like going out for a meal.

MOOD

Louise wasn't really .... going out for a meal.

30 'Last week, I unexpectedly met an old friend on the train,' said the man.

RUN

The man said that .... an old friend on the train unexpectedly last week.

Part 5

You are going to read an article about a flight in a very fast aeroplane. For questions **31–36**, choose the answer (**A**, **B**, **C** or **D**) which you think fits best according to the text.

Mark your answers **on the separate answer sheet**.

My fastest ever plane ride

Reporter Matt Rudd goes on an extraordinary plane ride

In The Red Bull Air Race, twelve pilots take it in turns to race through a series of pylons between 15 and 25 metres high, negotiating sharp turns, barrel rolls and loops on the way, all at speeds of up to 370 km per hour. I was invited to find out what it feels like to take part.

An hour before the flight, I had to sign two forms. The first confirmed that I was in good health, the second that I would empty all my pockets, because tiny objects can become very dangerous during the flight. I also learnt that I would have to try to stay orientated throughout. 'The horizon is your best friend,' I was told, 'the pilot will explain in which direction you have to look.' I was also asked to promise that when I was flying upside down, I would 'completely relax. Try and enjoy the view.' Half an hour before the flight, I had a safety briefing in which I was told not, under any circumstances, to touch anything.

By the time we were taxiing down the runway, my legs up in front of me, feet trying not to touch the incredibly important steering pedals, hands trying not to rest on any of the many important switches within reach, my mind had made itself up. Ignoring all instructions received, I would not relax and enjoy the flight. This is the cruel paradox of high-speed acrobatic flying. In order to survive it without passing out, you have to keep calm and focused. You have to tense up at the right time and you have to relax at the right time. Panicking is a bad idea. None of this was of particular comfort as we began accelerating down the runway.

Dario, the pilot, and I reached the end of the runway. There we were in the Zivko Edge 540, upsettingly one of the world's fastest acrobatic planes, ready to go. The plane took off and two seconds later we banked sharply to the right. It was an instant, violent manoeuvre and I felt the air squeeze out of my lungs. I looked up at the horizon, tensed everything and emitted short gasps as I sank down into the seat. For a split second I weighed 6.2 times my normal weight. And then we levelled out. We turned another sharp left and dived, leaving my stomach at 2,000 metres and my lungs scrunched up on the roof of the plane. Seconds later, we were 10 metres off the ground, aiming for the alarmingly small space between two pylons. They passed at 400 km per hour but my whoop of momentary excitement was stolen by a sharp right turn. We hadn't even done any acrobatics yet.   *line 55*
line 56

For two minutes, I was allowed to fly the plane, my hand shaking so much the plane shook too... it's that responsive. And then   *line 59* after that Dario said something. And I said, 'Can you repeat that?' But instead of replying, he did a barrel roll, a full lateral 360° turn.

'Are you okay?'

'Yup.'

'Have you had enough?'

'No,' I lied.

Then he did a loop, flying the plane up and over, turning a full circle in the air. Now, I am aware that many people would find this exciting. The sort of people who enjoy rollercoasters. However, I just thought it was   *line 71* a bit much. At the top of the loop, as we were flying upside down, I heard a small voice shouting, 'Relax, relax, look up.' Then I looked up and saw some fields.

The flight was over in 10 minutes. It had been 'soft' compared to what the pilots endure when they race. As if to illustrate the point, Dario got out some sandwiches the minute we landed and merrily tucked in. I didn't eat for hours and that night I did the loop the loop over and over again in my sleep.

31 How did Matt feel as the plane started moving along the runway?

    A annoyed that there were so many rules to follow

    B surprised that he had to sit in a rather awkward position

    C convinced that he was going to be unable to behave as required

    D anxious that he had not been adequately prepared for the experience

32 Why does Matt say *We hadn't even done any acrobatics yet* in lines 55 and 56?

    A to justify his impatience

    B to express his disappointment

    C to explain why he felt so relieved

    D to emphasise how apprehensive he felt

33 What does *responsive* mean in line 59?

    A eager

    B sensitive

    C active

    D helpful

34 In the fifth paragraph, Matt wants the pilot to think that

    A he understands the technical terms.

    B he needs a break.

    C he is feeling fine.

    D he had expected to roll.

35 What does *it* refer to in line 71?

    A turning a full circle

    B being aware

    C finding this exciting

    D enjoying rollercoasters

36 What is implied about the pilot in the final paragraph?

    A He finds Matt's reaction amusing.

    B He wants to demonstrate that he is tougher than Matt.

    C He feels unusually hungry after the flight.

    D He is completely unaffected by their experience.

Part 6

You are going to read an article about sleep and learning. Six sentences have been removed from the article. Choose from the sentences **A–G** the one which fits each gap (**37–42**). There is one extra sentence which you do not need to use.

Mark your answers **on the separate answer sheet**.

College students need their sleep!

Research into the connection between sleep and learning suggests that sleep is even more important than previously thought.

Only a month and a half into her first semester at college, Liz, a student at Harvard University, already wishes she had more time for sleep. Several mornings each week, Liz rises before six to join her teammates for rowing practice. On days like these she seldom sleeps more than seven hours per night, but it's not as if she doesn't try.

37 [ ] She often misses opportunities to socialize in order to get her coursework done and still get to bed at a reasonable time. Even without knowing just how important sleep is to learning, she tries to make time for it.

This is not always easy, however. The many demands on her time include her chosen sport, as well as activities like studying optional extra subjects. **38** [ ] She and other students who think the same way as her sacrifice sleep to fit everything in. It isn't surprising to learn, therefore, that students represent one of the most sleep-deprived segments of the population. Coursework, sports and new-found independence all contribute to the problem.

Studies have found that only eleven percent of college students sleep well consistently, while seventy-three percent experience at least occasional sleep issues, as Liz does. Forty percent of students felt well-rested no more than two days per week. Poor sleep is no longer considered a harmless aspect of college. **39** [ ] The results of this show that it has significant impact on memory and learning.

Inadequate sleep negatively affects our learning processes. It is simply more difficult to concentrate when we are sleep deprived; this affects our ability to focus on and gather information presented to us, and our ability to remember even those things we know we have learned in the past. **40** [ ] That is, the effect that many sleep researchers think it has on memory consolidation, the process by which connections in the brain strengthen and form into something more permanent.

A number of studies have shown that poor quality sleep can negatively impact on a person's ability to turn factual information or processes they've just learned into long-term memories. **41** [ ] And if this opportunity is missed – such as when a student stays awake all night – it generally can't be made up. Even if sleep is 'recovered' on subsequent nights, the brain will be less able to retain and make use of information gathered on the day before. These findings shed new light on the importance of making time for sleep, not only for college students like Liz, but for anyone who wants to continue to learn.

Early in her first semester at Harvard, Liz feels like she is maintaining a healthy balance, but only just. Trying hard to get the most out of her time in college, she admits it's sometimes hard to see sleep as an important part of her athletic and scholastic objectives. **42** [ ] Rather than thinking of sleep as wasted time or even time off, we should, they say, instead view it as the time when our brain is doing some of its most important work.

A Although it may seem unnecessary to do these, Liz views them as essential.

B It also has a less obvious but possibly even more profound impact.

C Liz knows that she must nevertheless do her best to avoid it.

D Research suggests that the most critical period of sleep for this to happen in is the one on the same day.

E In fact, Liz's behaviour is not at all like that of other college students her age.

F But that's exactly what many researchers say it is.

G Quite the opposite, actually, as research into its effects progresses.

Part 7

You are going to read an article in which four tourist guides talk about their work. For questions **43–52**, choose from the people (**A–D**). The people may be chosen more than once.

Mark your answers **on the separate answer sheet**.

Which person

says that a guide must be able to react to unexpected events?	**43**
takes clients to a location which is starting to disappear?	**44**
had a sudden realisation that he wanted to be a guide?	**45**
says he can look back on his experiences with pleasure?	**46**
fulfilled a long-held ambition?	**47**
admits to taking tourists on the wrong trip?	**48**
lived close to where history was made?	**49**
enjoys seeing his clients' sense of achievement?	**50**
criticises some of the people he guides?	**51**
mentions that his work changed someone's life for the better?	**52**

Adventure guides

*Four guides describe the benefits and drawbacks of taking tourists to
some of the world's most scenic, beautiful but different terrain.*

A Torfi from Iceland

The worst thing about being a guide in Iceland is when people haven't bothered to bring the right clothes for the weather. We like to say that there is no such thing as bad weather, only bad equipment. I haven't had any disasters but funny moments and blunders are endless: locking myself out of the car in a mind-numbing blizzard, taking folks hiking over a mountain when the schedule clearly said we should have been going rafting, being stranded on a glacier in a blizzard with a broken-down car for 16 hours. This is a job that provides a stream of good memories and friendship. The river Hvitá is my favourite place for white-water rafting. I'd also recommend a visit to the glacier to hike across the ice – you won't be able to do that for much longer as the ice is melting at an alarming rate.

B Tulga from Mongolia

When I became a guide I had virtually no training at all, just a two-hour lecture about what not to do. I had to learn from my mistakes. There were four Swiss people on my first trip. When I met them, I said: 'Hi guys.' They gave me a strange look. I asked if there was anything wrong but they said: 'No, no problem.' After two days, one of them explained, 'Guys means "goats" in our language.' I felt terrible. On a later trip, clients were upset because they were meant to see an ice gorge in the Gobi desert but our vehicle broke down and we didn't get there so they demanded half their money back. On a happier note, I once guided a family whose son had behavioural problems, and the child improved so much during the trip that a documentary was made about him called *The Horse Boy*.

C Ngima from Nepal

I used to watch the trekkers going through my village to the mountain peak situated just above it and that made me want to become a guide. The house where I grew up was on the old trekking path to Everest base camp. This is the route Sir Edmund Hillary and Sherpa Tenzing Norgay took to become the first people to climb Everest. We saw an inspiring video about them at school. On my first job as a lead guide, as we crossed the difficult Tashi Lapsa pass we had very heavy snowfall and one of our porters had to be rescued by helicopter because he got frostbite and snow-blindness. We have many beautiful places in Nepal but my favourite trek is up Mera Peak – from the summit you can see five mountains above 8,000m, including Everest.

D José from Peru

I was working in a factory when a school friend who was a river guide took me on an expedition. The moment our boat set off down the river I knew I had found the job for me. After two months of training, I guided my first group. Ten years later, one of my hands was badly damaged in an accident so it was impossible for me to continue. My boss suggested I use my legs rather than my arms, and this was the start of my life as a trek leader. You have to deal with lots of situations you hadn't anticipated would occur. There was the time when it snowed on the Inca Trail and the combination of snow and sun made for blinding conditions. So we had to improvise sunglasses out of the silver lining of our drinks boxes! I still love watching people's reactions on arriving at the summit of a high pass – it's so much better to get there after a few hours' walk than after a comfortable car journey.

WRITING (1 hour 20 minutes)

Part 1

You **must** answer this question. Write your answer in **140–190** words in an appropriate style **on the separate answer sheet**.

---

1   In your English class you have been talking about modern entertainment. Now, your English teacher has asked you to write an essay.

Write an essay using **all** the notes and giving reasons for your point of view.

Some people say that young people can only entertain themselves in front of a screen. What do you think?

Notes

Write about:

1.   why screen entertainment is so popular

2.   books and reading

3.   …(your own idea)

Part 2

Write an answer to **one** of the questions **2–4** in this part. Write your answer in **140–190** words in an appropriate style **on the separate answer sheet**. Put the question number in the box at the top of the answer sheet.

2   You have received an email from your English-speaking friend, Tom:

> As you know, my mum and dad own a restaurant and want me to work there when I leave college. However, I'm still really keen to be a journalist. What do you think I should do?

Write your **email**.

3   Your local government wants to improve your town centre and make it better for local people. Your college principal has asked students to write a report on the situation to send to the local government. In your report you should:

- Describe some of the problems in the town centre
- Suggest, with reasons, what improvements should be made to solve these problems

Write your **report**.

4   You see this notice in an English-language magazine:

> We're looking for articles about good luck.
>
> Write an article telling us about something lucky that happened to you and what effect this had.

Write your **article**.

LISTENING (approximately 40 minutes)

Part 1

You will hear people talking in eight different situations.

For questions **1–8**, choose the best answer (**A**, **B** or **C**).

---

1   You hear part of an interview with a crime writer.

What does he say about his home town?

A It was a good background for the writing he does.

B He generally feels uncomfortable returning there.

C People there tend to treat him differently now.

2   You hear a careers adviser talking to a woman who has applied for two jobs.

What suggestion does he make?

A find out more information about the first job

B withdraw the application for the second job

C ask the first company to be flexible

3   You hear a girl talking about a psychology textbook.

What does she say about it?

A It is not very interesting.

B It is good value for money.

C It is going to come in useful.

4   You hear the mother of a famous skier talking about a competition.

She says that her daughter

A expected to win the competition.

B didn't tell her mother she was entering it.

C gave up her job to practise for it.

5 You hear a film director talking about the actors she works with.

How does she feel about the actors in her current film?

A She sympathises with their problems.

B She admires the sacrifices they make.

C She approves of their attitudes.

6 You hear a man talking about his first job interview.

How did he feel during the interview?

A confident that he was right for the job

B embarrassed because of the long silences

C relieved he could answer most of the questions

7 You hear two friends talking about a popular television programme.

What is the programme about?

A retirement

B cookery

C teaching

8 You hear two people talking about a place they have visited.

What kind of place is it?

A a museum

B a library

C a shop

Part 2

You will hear a girl called Laura Beamer talking about being a volunteer at a summer school for 7–14 year olds, which is called the Children's University. For questions **9–18**, complete the sentences with a word or short phrase.

Volunteer at the Children's University

The Children's University was started by a [_____ **9**] five years ago.

The focus of this year's Children's University was the topic of [_____ **10**] .

Laura's partner was Mark, who works as a [_____ **11**] when he is not volunteering.

Laura's group of volunteers gave some workshops about how [_____ **12**] is made.

Laura says the children had a booklet called a '[_____ **13**]' which was stamped to show their progress.

Laura and the children went to the graduation ceremony in the [_____ **14**] hall of the local University.

Some children received a [_____ **15**] for attending a lot of workshops.

Laura said the scheme allowed her to develop skills such as [_____ **16**] .

Laura will most probably become a [_____ **17**] in the future.

Laura says she can give people in her audience something called an [_____ **18**] for volunteers.

Part 3

You will hear five different people talking about why they have applied to go on a space journey to the planet Mars. For questions **19–23**, choose from the list (**A–H**) each speaker's reason for applying to go on the trip to Mars. Use the letters only once. There are three extra letters which you do not need to use.

A   to discover new natural resources

B   to learn new skills

Speaker 1   **19**

C   to take advantage of a rare opportunity

Speaker 2   **20**

D   to be involved in advancing scientific knowledge

Speaker 3   **21**

E   to become a famous personality

Speaker 4   **22**

F   to face an extreme challenge

Speaker 5   **23**

G   to provide others with inspiration

H   to be among the first to have the experience

Part 4

You will hear an interview with a man called Mark Phillips, who is talking about his work as a potter. For questions **24–30**, choose the best answer (**A**, **B** or **C**).

24   Why did pottery not appeal to Mark when he was younger?

    A   He was put off by his mother's achievements.

    B   His many attempts always seemed to end in failure.

    C   He was too busy playing in a band to take an interest.

25   Why did Mark decide to take up pottery?

    A   His business wasn't as successful as he wanted it to be.

    B   He saw how enjoyable pottery classes could be.

    C   He realised he needed to be more creative.

26   What did Mark say about being a student again?

    A   He missed having responsibility.

    B   He was made to feel that he was different.

    C   He felt physically challenged.

27   Mark describes the pots he makes as

    A   reflecting shapes in nature.

    B   objects that are to be used.

    C   similar to his mother's in design.

28   What has surprised Mark about the pottery community?

    A   how supportive they have been to a newcomer

    B   how willing other potters are to share ideas

    C   how content they are with their lifestyle

29 What advice from his mother has Mark valued most?

    A to concentrate all his efforts on perfecting pottery

    B to remember the skill of potters from the past

    C to be realistic about the money-making possibilities of pottery

30 In the future, Mark says he would like to be able to

    A develop some new colours for his pots.

    B exhibit his pots in a gallery.

    C explore different techniques for making pots.

SPEAKING (14 minutes)

You take the Speaking test with another candidate (possibly two candidates), referred to here as your partner. There are two examiners. One will speak to you and your partner and the other will be listening. Both examiners will award marks.

Part 1 (2 minutes)

The examiner asks you and your partner questions about yourselves. You may be asked about things like 'your home town', 'your interests', 'your career plans', etc.

Part 2 (a one-minute 'long turn' for each candidate, plus a 30-second response from the second candidate)

The examiner gives you two photographs and asks you to talk about them for one minute. The examiner then asks your partner a question about your photographs and your partner responds briefly.

Then the examiner gives your partner two different photographs. Your partner talks about these photographs for one minute. This time the examiner asks you a question about your partner's photographs and you respond briefly.

Part 3 (4 minutes)

The examiner asks you and your partner to talk together. They give you a task to look at so you can think about and discuss an idea, giving reasons for your opinion. For example, you may be asked to think about some changes in the world, or about spending free time with your family. After you have discussed the task for about two minutes with your partner, the examiner will ask you a follow-up question, which you should discuss for a further minute.

Part 4 (4 minutes)

The examiner asks some further questions, which leads to a more general discussion of what you have talked about in Part 3. You may comment on your partner's answers if you wish.

Test 6

READING AND USE OF ENGLISH (1 hour 15 minutes)

Part 1

For questions **1–8**, read the text below and decide which answer (**A**, **B**, **C** or **D**) best fits each gap. There is an example at the beginning (**0**).

Mark your answers **on the separate answer sheet**.

Example:

0 **A** open   **B** think   **C** find   **D** look

0	A	B	C	D
	▭	▭	▬	▭

The importance of science

The aim of science is to **(0)** .... out how the world and everything in it, and beyond it, works. Some people, though, **(1)** .... that much of what is done in the name of science is a waste of time and money. What is the **(2)** .... in investigating how atoms behave or in studying stars billions of kilometres away? Science, they argue, is of **(3)** .... only if it has some practical use.

When the Scottish scientist James Clerk Maxwell **(4)** .... experiments with electricity and magnetism in the late 19th century, he had no particular end in **(5)** .... and was certainly not **(6)** .... to make money; he was simply trying to reveal more about how the world works. And yet his work laid the **(7)** .... for our modern way of life. Computers, the internet, satellites, mobile phones, televisions, medical scanners all owe their existence to the fact that a scientist **(8)** .... the need to understand the world a little better.

1	**A** claim	**B** demand	**C** tell	**D** review
2	**A** basis	**B** cause	**C** point	**D** sake
3	**A** gain	**B** profit	**C** advantage	**D** value
4	**A** brought on	**B** carried out	**C** pulled out	**D** set off
5	**A** plan	**B** idea	**C** mind	**D** thought
6	**A** reaching	**B** aiming	**C** targeting	**D** designing
7	**A** sources	**B** origins	**C** structures	**D** foundations
8	**A** held	**B** felt	**C** chose	**D** used

Part 2

For questions **9–16**, read the text below and think of the word which best fits each gap. Use only **one** word in each gap. There is an example at the beginning (**0**).

Write your answers **IN CAPITAL LETTERS on the separate answer sheet**.

Example: | 0 | | O | F | | | | | | | | | | | | | | | | |

Food preservation

Keeping food for long periods **(0)** .... time was historically a huge problem. This proved especially crucial **(9)** .... times when agricultural production **(10)** .... severely limited by weather or crop failure. People commonly used ice to keep food fresh but, of **(11)** .... , ice itself melts relatively quickly. In 1859 an American, John Mason, invented a glass jar with a metal screw-on lid, creating a perfect seal and making **(12)** .... possible to preserve food that would previously not have remained edible. Mason's jar is still **(13)** .... use throughout the world.

An even **(14)** .... successful method for keeping food by canning it in metal containers was perfected between 1870 **(15)** .... 1920 by Englishman Bryan Donkin. This preserved food beautifully, though the early iron cans were expensive, heavy and difficult to open. A breakthrough came in the 1880s with the development of lighter materials **(16)** .... also enabled mass production of cans.

Part 3

For questions **17–24**, read the text below. Use the word given in capitals at the end of some of the lines to form a word that fits in the gap **in the same line**. There is an example at the beginning **(0)**.

Write your answers **IN CAPITAL LETTERS on the separate answer sheet**.

Example: | 0 | P | A | R | T | I | C | U | L | A | R | L | Y | | | | | | |

Enjoying travel

I always enjoy travelling, **(0)** .... when it means visiting other countries. One of the clearest memories from my childhood is of going to Disneyworld. Some people disapprove of the place but I loved it as a child and found it just as **(17)** .... when I returned years later as an adult.

PARTICULAR

ENJOY

I am **(18)** .... that my work involves a lot of travel. The two places I visit most often are Barcelona and New York. I like both, but there is a tremendous **(19)** .... between them. Barcelona is relaxed and overflowing with culture. New York, though, is bustling and full of **(20)** .... When I'm there I'm constantly looking upwards, overwhelmed by the **(21)** .... of the buildings. It is quite **(22)** .... anywhere else I've ever been.

FORTUNE

DIFFERENT

EXCITE

HIGH

LIKE

I went to Tokyo last year and found it absolutely fascinating. However, my top **(23)** .... for a city break has to be Toronto; it is visually **(24)** .... and I've had some of the best meals I've ever eaten there.

CHOOSE

SPECTACLE

Part 4

For questions **25–30**, complete the second sentence so that it has a similar meaning to the first sentence, using the word given. **Do not change the word given**. You must use between **two** and **five** words, including the word given. Here is an example (**0**).

Example:

0   A very friendly taxi driver drove us into town.

DRIVEN

We .... a very friendly taxi driver.

The gap can be filled by the words 'were driven into town by', so you write:

Example:	**0**	*WERE DRIVEN INTO TOWN BY*

Write **only** the missing words **IN CAPITAL LETTERS on the separate answer sheet**.

---

25   Everyone apart from John thought that Lisa would get the job.

PERSON

John was .... not expect Lisa to get the job.

26   I'm concerned about whether I'll be able to finish the project on time.

CONCERNS

What .... whether I'll be able to finish the project on time.

27   We had to leave the lecture early or we would have missed the last bus.

UNTIL

If we .... of the lecture, we would have missed the last bus.

28 The number of students going to university went up last year.

INCREASE

There .... the number of students going to university last year.

29 I'll phone you tonight so you can tell me what you've been doing.

CATCH

I'll phone you tonight to .... news.

30 That was one of the best meals I've had this year.

AS

I've had very .... that one this year.

Part 5

You are going to read an article about a wildlife cameraman called Doug Allan. For questions **31–36**, choose the answer (**A**, **B**, **C** or **D**) which you think fits best according to the text.

Mark your answers **on the separate answer sheet**.

Wildlife cameraman

Doug Allan films wild animals in cold places. If you've ever been amazed by footage of polar bears in a nature documentary, it's probably been filmed by him. His perfect temperature, he says, is -18°C. Allan trained as a marine biologist and commercial diver. Diving was his first passion, where he learned about survival in cold places. His big break came when a TV crew turned up in Antarctica, where Allan was working, to film a wildlife documentary. 'I ended up taking the crew to different places, and after 48 hours I realised that being a wildlife cameraman ticked all the boxes: travel, adventure, underwater.'

He is now a top cameraman and has worked on many major TV wildlife series. 'I came along at a good time. When I started, hardly anyone had been to the Antarctic. You had coral people, elephant people, chimpanzee people. I just became the cold man. It was like all these amazing sequences were just waiting to be captured on film.' The camera and communications technology was very basic when he started 35 years ago. 'It is certainly easier to film today. If you shot something then, you had to remember it. Today, with digital technology, you can shoot a lot and look at it immediately. You used to have to think what shots you needed next, and what you had missed. You shot less. Film was very expensive. Today you can have too much material.'

'My value is field experience in cold conditions. I have a feel for it. I have spent so much time on sea ice it now feels like crossing the street. I do get cold toes but the poles are healthy places. There are no leeches, no diseases or mosquitoes.' Wildlife filming, Allan says, is full of great successes, but also failures and embarrassments. Once, he was in the Orkneys to film kittiwakes. Unfortunately he could not identify which birds they were.

When Allan recently got permission to film sequences for a major TV series in Kong Karls Land, a group of islands in the Arctic Ocean, he did not expect an easy assignment. It is a world of polar bears and is strictly off limits to all but the most fearless or foolish. Usually -32°C in April, the wind is vicious and hauling cameras in the deep snow is a nightmare. After walking five or more hours a day and watching polar bear dens in the snow slopes for 23 days, however, Allan had seen just one mother bear and her cub. By day 24, though, he says, he was living in bear world, at bear speed, with bear senses.

'We find a new hole and wait. We shuffle, hop, bend, stretch and run to stay warm. Five hours of watching and then with no warning at all I catch a glimpse so brief that I almost miss it. But the camera's locked on the hole on full zoom and my eye's very quickly on the viewfinder. Nothing for a couple of seconds and then an unmistakable black nose. Nose becomes muzzle, grows bigger to become full head and in less than a minute she has her front legs out and is resting on the snow in front of the hole. She's looking at me but she's not bothered. I've just taken a close-up, thinking this can't get much better ... when she sets off on a long slide down the slope. I'd swear it's partly in sheer pleasure,' he recounts, adding that two cubs then appeared at the den entrance. 'Clearly it's their first view of the world ... It's show time on the slopes and we have front-row seats.'

Now Allan would like to make his own film about climate change in the Arctic, talking to the people who live there and experience the impact of it first hand. He says he would be *line 80* able to make an extraordinary documentary.

31 What do we learn about Allan in the first paragraph?

    A He had to train as a diver in order to become a wildlife cameraman.
    B Becoming a cameraman suited the interests he already had.
    C He was given the chance to work as a cameraman by a TV crew he met.
    D Finding work as a cameraman allowed him to remain in Antarctica.

32 What does Allan say about the first documentaries he worked on?

    A He has very clear memories of them.
    B Most of what he filmed was new to viewers.
    C They were shorter than those he makes nowadays.
    D He would have liked to have been able to choose where he worked.

33 Why does Allan compare spending time on sea ice to crossing the street?

    A It is an ordinary occurrence for him.
    B He thinks it presents a similar level of danger.
    C He has learnt to approach it in the same way.
    D It requires skills that can be used in winter conditions anywhere.

34 When Allan had been on Kong Karls Land for a while, he began to

    A stop worrying about the dangers he was facing.
    B feel a deep understanding of how polar bears lived.
    C get used to the terrible conditions for filming.
    D be more hopeful that one bear would lead him to others.

35 What feeling does Allan describe in the fifth paragraph?

    A panic when he nearly fails to film a fantastic sequence
    B concern that he has disturbed an adult female with her young
    C amazement at being lucky enough to capture some great shots
    D delight at being able to move around after waiting quietly for ages

36 What does *it* refer to in line 80?

    A Allan's film
    B climate change
    C the Arctic
    D living there

Part 6

You are going to read an article about how the Egyptian pyramids were built. Six sentences have been removed from the article. Choose from the sentences **A–G** the one which fits each gap (**37–42**). There is one extra sentence which you do not need to use.

Mark your answers **on the separate answer sheet**.

Has one of the mysteries of the ancient pyramids been solved?

A painting in a 3000-year-old tomb suggests how the Ancient Egyptians may have transported the heavy stones used to build the pyramids.

Ever since the discovery of the first pyramid, scientists have wondered how ancient Egyptians built these monumental structures that are visible even from space.

There are a number of theories about the construction techniques they used. **37** Egyptologists had always wondered how workers were able to move the giant limestone blocks. These weigh as much as 2.5 tons each, and the stone quarries from which they were cut were often located hundreds of kilometres away from the pyramid sites.

Dragging them on basic wooden sledges, similar to those people use to slide down snow-covered slopes in winter, was the obvious answer. **38** It now turns out that the workers probably did have some assistance – from ordinary water! What is even more amazing is that the answer to the Egyptologists' puzzle has been staring them in the face for many years, in a wall painting in the tomb of an ancient Egyptian king, or pharaoh.

The artwork, which depicts a pharaoh being pulled along by a large team of workers, has one significant detail that had so far been misinterpreted – a man pouring water in front of the sledge the pharaoh is being dragged upon. Egyptologists had always thought that the man was performing some kind of religious ritual. However, some scientists now believe that the water was being poured for a totally different reason. **39**

This revelation was made by researchers from the University of Amsterdam and the Foundation for Fundamental Research on Matter. The scientists arrived at this conclusion after conducting extensive testing in their laboratory, by sliding a weighted tray across both dry sand and sand that had been mixed with varying amounts of water. In dry sand, heaps formed in front of the tray as it was dragged along. **40**

However, as the researchers added water, the sand hardened, which helped reduce both the force needed to pull the tray and the friction against it. That's because the water helps form tiny water bridges, known as capillary bridges, between the sand particles, causing them to stick together. **41** The force required to pull the sledge would have been reduced by as much as 50% as the sand became stiffer, which meant that half as many workers were needed to move the heavy stones.

There was a tipping point, though. After the moisture exceeded a certain amount, the stiffness started to decrease and the capillary bridges melted away, causing the sand to clump up around the tray once again. According to the researchers, the perfect balance appears to be when the volume of the water is between 2 – 5% of the volume of sand. **42** And so another step has been taken towards understanding the incredible feat achieved by these ancient engineers. Now if we could only find a painting that would tell us how the workers erected these impressive structures without access to modern mechanics, that would be amazing!

A However, to do so would have required superhuman strength against the friction of the desert sand.

B This allowed them to work out exactly how much of it had been used every time.

C This slowed it down dramatically.

D One question, however, had been left unanswered.

E The pyramid builders seem to have realised that this was the correct proportion.

F The effect of this turns out to be significant.

G It was to help the sledge move more easily across the sand.

Part 7

You are going to read four reviews of books about sleep and dreams. For questions **43–52**, choose from the reviews (**A–D**). The reviews may be chosen more than once.

Mark your answers **on the separate answer sheet**.

Which review

emphasises how enjoyable sleep is?	**43**
says certain aspects of our lives are becoming less distinct from one another?	**44**
points out that many people share a mistaken belief?	**45**
describes the structure of the book?	**46**
explains why we have certain experiences?	**47**
mentions a practical problem faced by scientists?	**48**
says the book shows that major developments have occurred in a field?	**49**
says the writer deals with issues that cause debate?	**50**
comments that our lack of knowledge regarding sleep is surprising?	**51**
says the reader learns how a technological advance caused problems?	**52**

Four books about sleep

A Sleepfaring

Why do we sleep? Are we sleeping enough? How can we tackle sleep problems? Jim Horne finds answers to these questions and many more in *Sleepfaring*, a journey through the science and the secrets of sleep. He reveals what goes on in our brains during sleep, and also gives some hints from the latest sleep research that may just help you get a better night's rest. In recent years, understanding sleep has become increasingly important, as people work longer hours, styles of working have altered, and the separation between workplace and home is being reduced by cell phones and the internet. Horne draws on the latest research to reveal what science has discovered about sleep. Nor does Horne avoid controversial topics; challenging, for example, the conventional wisdom on the amount of sleep we actually need. For anyone wishing to know more about the many mysterious processes that begin when we close our eyes each night, *Sleepfaring* offers a wealth of insight and information.

B Dreaming

What is dreaming? Why are dreams so strange and why are they so hard to remember? In this fascinating book, Harvard researcher Allan Hobson offers an intriguing look at our nightly journey through the world of dreams. He describes how the theory of dreaming has advanced dramatically. We have learned that, in dreaming, some areas of the brain are very active – the visual and auditory centres, for instance – while others are completely shut down, including the centres for self-awareness, logic, and memory. Thus we can have visually vivid dreams, but be utterly unaware that the sequence of events or localities may be bizarre and, quite often, impossible. And because the memory centre is inactive, we don't remember the dream at all, unless we wake up while it is in progress. With special boxed features that highlight intriguing questions – Do we dream in colour? (yes), Do animals dream? (probably) – *Dreaming* offers a cutting-edge account of the most mysterious area of our mental life.

C Counting Sheep

Even though we will devote a third of our lives to sleep, we still know remarkably little about its origins and purpose. Does getting up early really benefit us? Can some people really exist on just a few hours' sleep a night? Does everybody dream? Do fish dream? How did people cope before alarm clocks and caffeine? And is anybody getting enough sleep? Paul Martin's *Counting Sheep* answers these questions and more in this illuminating work of popular science. Even the wonders of yawning are explained in full. To sleep, to dream: *Counting Sheep* reflects the centrality of these activities to our lives and can help readers respect, understand, and appreciate that delicious time when they're lost to the world.

D Dreamland

Reporter Randall provides a brisk tour of sleep research and what it means for individuals hoping to feel well rested. The author engaged with sleep research in part because of his sleepwalking. Researching the world of sleep is obviously difficult because sleeping subjects selected for studies rarely remember anything specific. Nonetheless, Randall interviewed sleep researchers and read academic papers to learn what he could from those who devote their careers to the science of sleep. The book is not a continuous narrative but rather a loose progression of chapters about different sleep-related issues. For example, Randall explains how the invention of electricity led to countless cases of sleep deprivation; the lack of utter darkness after sunset is often the enemy of sound sleep. He also emphasises the too-often neglected common-sense realisation that sleep is no void; rather, it is perhaps one third of the puzzle of living well.

WRITING (1 hour 20 minutes)

Part 1

You **must** answer this question. Write your answer in **140–190** words in an appropriate style **on the separate answer sheet**.

---

1   In your English class you have been talking about education. Now, your English teacher has asked you to write an essay.

Write an essay using **all** the notes and giving reasons for your point of view.

'Teachers need more than just a good knowledge of their subject.'
What do you think?

Notes

Write about:

1. patience

2. friendliness

3. ...(your own idea)

Part 2

Write an answer to **one** of the questions **2–4** in this part. Write your answer in **140–190** words in an appropriate style **on the separate answer sheet**. Put the question number in the box at the top of the answer sheet.

2   You have received an email from your English-speaking friend, Robert:

> Hi!
>
> My parents are both 50 next month and I want to do something special for them – I can't decide whether to organise a surprise birthday party or take them away to a hotel for the weekend. What do you think I should do?

Write your **email**.

3   You recently saw this notice on an English-language website called *TV Watch*:

> *Reviews wanted!*
>
> # TV series
>
> Is there a TV series which you watch regularly?
>
> Write a review of the series explaining what it is about, why you like it and who you would recommend it to.

Write your **review**.

4   You see this advertisement on your college noticeboard:

> **Wanted: English-speaking guide**
>
> A group of English students is coming to your town for a week. The tourist office is looking for a guide to show the students the town. Write a letter of application to the organizer of the tour, Mrs Isobel Parks, explaining:
> - Which places you would take the students to visit
> - Why you would be the best person for the job

Write your **letter**.

LISTENING (approximately 40 minutes)

Part 1

You will hear people talking in eight different situations.

For questions **1–8**, choose the best answer (**A**, **B** or **C**).

1   You hear a psychologist talking about green spaces in cities.

    What does she say about them?

    A People fail to appreciate them as much as they should.

    B They are more important for children than for adults.

    C Few governments make them a priority.

2   You hear part of an interview with a singer.

    What does he say about playing tennis?

    A It calms him down after a performance.

    B It is used by a lot of singers to improve their technique.

    C It requires similar skills to singing.

3   You hear an actor talking about how she met her husband.

    How did she first meet him?

    A She sat next to him in a cinema.

    B She appeared in a play with him.

    C A friend introduced them.

4   You hear two people talking about a bus service.

    What does the man say about it?

    A It is frequent.

    B It is cheap.

    C It is punctual.

5   You hear a retired ballerina comparing dancers today with dancers in the past.

She says professional ballet dancers today

   A   are less concerned about expressing emotion.

   B   are more interested in being celebrities.

   C   dance with less technical ability.

6   You hear a chef talking about making a TV series.

What does he say about it?

   A   He didn't expect to enjoy the experience so much.

   B   He didn't get on with his co-presenter.

   C   He didn't like the working hours.

7   You hear two friends talking about an art course.

What do they agree about it?

   A   The teacher is inspiring.

   B   The class is the right size.

   C   The content is interesting.

8   You hear a swimmer talking about a competition she took part in.

How does she feel about it?

   A   disappointed with her result

   B   excited about where it will lead

   C   surprised by the support she received

Part 2

You will hear a man called Sid Holmes talking about a journalism course he attended. For questions **9–18**, complete the sentences with a word or short phrase.

Journalism Course

Sid did the same course in journalism that his [9] did.

On the first day, Sid had to do a reporting exercise about a man who was rescued from a [10] by helicopter.

An assistant editor from the [11] section of a local newspaper gave an interesting talk about being a journalist.

Sid's main tutor had written a biography of a famous local [12] .

Sid had an idea for an article about a man who makes [13] for young people to borrow.

Sid's first article was published in a [14] soon after he wrote it.

Sid had to report on a council meeting about proposed improvements to the [15] in the town.

One aspect of the course Sid didn't enjoy was the [16] classes.

Sid found it useful to chat to his classmates in the [17] at the college.

Sid now has a chance of getting a job at a [18] .

Part 3

You will hear five short extracts in which people are talking about collecting things as a hobby. For questions **19–23**, choose from the list (**A–H**) why each speaker collects the things. Use the letters only once. There are three extra letters which you do not need to use.

A   I enjoy the challenge.

B   It means I spend time with my family.

Speaker 1 | **19**

C   It's a way of meeting interesting people.

Speaker 2 | **20**

D   I want to help the local community.

Speaker 3 | **21**

E   I use my collection to teach other people.

Speaker 4 | **22**

F   It's a financial investment.

Speaker 5 | **23**

G   It connects me to the past.

H   I like to have beautiful things around me.

Part 4

You will hear an interview with a scientist called Peter Crane, who is talking about an ancient tree called the gingko. For questions **24–30**, choose the best answer (**A**, **B** or **C**).

24 What first interested Peter about the gingko tree?

    A how its leaves grow

    B the family it belongs to

    C what's known about its history

25 What does Peter say about the gingko tree in ancient China?

    A It wasn't originally grown for its nuts.

    B It wasn't common before people started growing it.

    C It was one of the earliest plants to be grown there.

26 When asked about the medicinal uses of gingko, Peter says

    A researchers in different parts of the world disagree about it.

    B scientists have failed to identify any positive effects.

    C some parts of the plant help the brain to function.

27 Why are there so many gingko trees in cities all over the world?

    A They don't suffer from problems that usually affect trees there.

    B Other trees can't survive if they are too close to the species.

    C People take more trouble to look after them than other trees.

28 Peter says that street trees benefit people by providing

    A some protection from the sun.

    B a reduction in traffic noise.

    C increased privacy.

29 Peter says people can help other species of plant to survive by

    A leaving plants to grow in the wild.

    B protecting them from plant-eating animals.

    C growing them in many different places.

30 How does Peter's work influence the way he thinks about the world?

    A It makes him feel concerned about the future of human beings.

    B It reminds him that human beings are a relatively new species.

    C It allows him to understand why human beings focus on the present.

SPEAKING (14 minutes)

You take the Speaking test with another candidate (possibly two candidates), referred to here as your partner. There are two examiners. One will speak to you and your partner and the other will be listening. Both examiners will award marks.

Part 1 (2 minutes)

The examiner asks you and your partner questions about yourselves. You may be asked about things like 'your home town', 'your interests', 'your career plans', etc.

Part 2 (a one-minute 'long turn' for each candidate, plus a 30-second response from the second candidate)

The examiner gives you two photographs and asks you to talk about them for one minute. The examiner then asks your partner a question about your photographs and your partner responds briefly.

Then the examiner gives your partner two different photographs. Your partner talks about these photographs for one minute. This time the examiner asks you a question about your partner's photographs and you respond briefly.

Part 3 (4 minutes)

The examiner asks you and your partner to talk together. They give you a task to look at so you can think about and discuss an idea, giving reasons for your opinion. For example, you may be asked to think about some changes in the world, or about spending free time with your family. After you have discussed the task for about two minutes with your partner, the examiner will ask you a follow-up question, which you should discuss for a further minute.

Part 4 (4 minutes)

The examiner asks some further questions, which leads to a more general discussion of what you have talked about in Part 3. You may comment on your partner's answers if you wish.

Test 7

READING AND USE OF ENGLISH (1 hour 15 minutes)

Part 1

For questions **1–8**, read the text below and decide which answer (**A, B, C** or **D**) best fits each gap. There is an example at the beginning (**0**).

Mark your answers **on the separate answer sheet**.

Example:

0   A settled   **B** established   **C** installed   **D** found

```
  ┌──────────────────────────────┐
  │       A    B    C    D        │
  │ 0                             │
  │      ▭    ▬    ▭    ▭         │
  └──────────────────────────────┘
```

A new partnership

In 1884, a small engineering firm was **(0)** .... in a part of Manchester. Its owner had **(1)** .... to complete only two years in formal education yet was still successfully **(2)** .... a business. In 1903, he bought his first car but it did not meet his high **(3)** .... and, being an engineer, he could not **(4)** .... having a go at improving it. By the following year he had designed a new car himself, and then started manufacturing this model. One of his cars came to the **(5)** .... of a wealthy car salesman from an aristocratic background. He was **(6)** .... impressed by the car and a meeting was **(7)** .... between the two of them at the Midland Hotel in Manchester. The meeting was a success and the two men decided to go into business together. The name of the manufacturer was Henry Royce and that of the wealthy aristocrat, Charles Rolls – and so the world-famous brand, the luxurious Rolls-Royce, was **(8)** ....

1 **A** passed   **B** achieved   **C** managed   **D** allowed

2 **A** arranging   **B** running   **C** working   **D** dealing

3 **A** standards   **B** rates   **C** levels   **D** ranks

4 **A** obstruct   **B** resist   **C** oppose   **D** refuse

5 **A** attention   **B** view   **C** interest   **D** attraction

6 **A** widely   **B** mainly   **C** greatly   **D** fully

7 **A** put out   **B** turned up   **C** taken out   **D** set up

8 **A** brought   **B** originated   **C** discovered   **D** born

Part 2

For questions **9–16**, read the text below and think of the word which best fits each gap. Use only **one** word in each gap. There is an example at the beginning (**0**).

Write your answers **IN CAPITAL LETTERS on the separate answer sheet**.

Example: | 0 | | F | O | R | | | | | | | | | | | | | | |

The importance of reading

Reading is good (**0**) .... us. In fact, there is plenty of evidence that reading for pleasure is more than just another leisure pursuit – it actually improves our mental and physical health. Reading extended texts (**9**) .... as novels or biographies, (**10**) .... requires intense concentration for a considerable period of time, helps to lengthen attention spans in children and improves their ability to think clearly. However, experts say (**11**) .... is essential to acquire the habit of reading extensively (**12**) .... a small child, while the brain is still developing.

Reading can undoubtedly (**13**) .... beneficial to our mental well-being. Reading not (**14**) .... helps combat feelings of loneliness, it also allows people to relax and forget their problems for (**15**) .... while. The concentration required during the act of reading seems to ease muscle tension and slow the heart rate. Researchers have found that just six minutes of reading can reduce stress levels by as (**16**) .... as two-thirds.

Part 3

For questions **17–24**, read the text below. Use the word given in capitals at the end of some of the lines to form a word that fits in the gap **in the same line**. There is an example at the beginning (**0**).

Write your answers **IN CAPITAL LETTERS on the separate answer sheet**.

Example: | 0 | E | X | P | E | N | S | I | V | E | | | | | | | | |

The price of meals

When a meal is **(0)** .... , do people say they enjoy it simply because   **EXPENSE**

it costs a lot of money? There is some **(17)** .... from an experiment   **EVIDENT**

in a New York restaurant which suggests that this might be so.

The restaurant served diners a meal but charged some **(18)** ....   **TWO**

as much as others, even though the meals were identical and taken

in the same **(19)** .... with the same level of service. After the meal   **SURROUND**

everyone was asked what they thought of the meal. One might think

that the people who had paid least would be the most impressed with

the meal. **(20)** .... though, it was those who had paid most who   **SURPRISE**

gave it the highest **(21)** ....   **RATE**

According to a well-known **(22)** .... the reason for this finding is   **PSYCHOLOGY**

that a high price for a meal is very **(23)** .... in convincing people   **SIGNIFY**

that a meal is good. One wonders if this might **(24)** .... restaurant   **COURAGE**

owners to keep their prices high.

Part 4

For questions **25–30**, complete the second sentence so that it has a similar meaning to the first sentence, using the word given. **Do not change the word given.** You must use between **two** and **five** words, including the word given. Here is an example (**0**).

Example:

0   A very friendly taxi driver drove us into town.

DRIVEN

We .... a very friendly taxi driver.

The gap can be filled by the words 'were driven into town by', so you write:

Example:	0	*WERE DRIVEN INTO TOWN BY*

Write **only** the missing words **IN CAPITAL LETTERS on the separate answer sheet.**

---

25   Last Saturday my friend asked me, 'Do you want to see a film tonight?'

WHETHER

Last Saturday my friend asked me .... a film that night.

26   The journey was shorter than I had expected.

LONG

The journey was .... I had expected.

27   'There's been a rise of over ten per cent in the price of the tickets,' said Sue.

GONE

Sue said that the price of the tickets .... than ten per cent this year.

28 He sings in the show and dances in it as well.

ONLY

Not .... in the show, he also dances in it.

29 My mother thought it would be good for me to live abroad for some time.

BENEFIT

My mother thought that I would .... abroad for some time.

30 I am sorry I didn't contact you, but I was very busy.

TOUCH

I apologise for .... you, but I was very busy.

Part 5

You are going to read an extract from a book about a cycle ride from Russia to the UK. For questions **31–36**, choose the answer (**A**, **B**, **C** or **D**) which you think fits best according to the text.

Mark your answers **on the separate answer sheet**.

Cycling Home from Siberia, by Robert Lilwall

We had been flying east all night and I awoke to notice that it was already daylight. Looking out of the window onto the empty landscape below, the dark shades of brown and green reassured me that, although it was mid-September, it had not yet started snowing in Siberia. I could see no sign of human life and the view rolled away in an otherworldly blend of mountains, streams and forests to an endless horizon.

My Russian neighbour Sergei woke up and smiled at me sleepily. I had told him that I was flying to the far-eastern Siberian city of Magadan with only a one-way ticket because it was my intention to return home to England by bicycle. 'But, Robert,' he had reasoned with me, 'there is no road from Magadan; you cannot ride a bicycle.' I explained that I had reason to believe that there was a road, though not many people used it these days.

'Alone?' he asked, pointing at me.

'No, I will be riding with a friend called Al.'

'Just one friend?'

'Yes just one,' I nodded. Sergei still looked unconvinced and with just one word 'Holodna' (cold) he pointed outside. I tried to
line 27 bolster my case by explaining to Sergei with hand gestures that I had a lot of warm clothes, though I left out the fact that, because my trip was self-funded I was on a tight budget. Most of my clothes and equipment had been bought at slashed prices. In reality, I was not at all sure they would be up to the job. This was especially true of my enormous postman's over-trousers which I had bought for £10.

My life of travel had all started in a lecture hall in Scotland several years ago. The hall that morning was full of students slumped in their seats. Some were taking notes, without energy. The lecturer droned on. I was thinking hard about a particular dilemma. Should I ask him or not? 'Well, why not?' I tore a fresh sheet from my pad and wrote, 'Hi Al, Do you want to cycle across the Karakorum Highway between Pakistan and China this summer? Rob.' In the row in front of me slouched Al, my old school friend. I tapped him on the shoulder and passed the note. He tried to decipher my scrawl, scratched his head, wrote something and passed it back. I unfolded it and held my breath while I read. 'OK,' it said.

Six years later I was going to join Al in Siberia. I had been working as a geography teacher and although I was still far from having full control of my classes, the job did tick many important boxes for me. It was frequently challenging, rarely boring, often fulfilling and of course there were great long holidays in which to chase adventures. Twice since I had started teaching I had used these holidays to go to meet Al. He had caught the adventuring-bug in a big way after our bike ride through Pakistan and so had decided to do something far more relaxing than teaching: to cycle around the world. I was now joining him for the Siberian part of his trip.

Ever since that first ride we had taken together, Al had been setting himself greater and greater challenges. This round-the-world-by-bike trip was certainly his greatest so far. At times he thought that the ride, or the road, would break him. Although it sounded tough, I envied him in many ways. He was having an extraordinary adventure, finding that he could deal with each new challenge even if it seemed impossible. He was proving wrong the sceptics who had told him he could not do it. He was doing something that scared him nearly every day and it made him feel alive.

31 In the opening paragraph Robert reveals that he was

    A grateful that the long night was over.

    B relieved that the winter weather had not yet arrived.

    C surprised that the area seemed uninhabited.

    D disappointed by the colours of the earth below him.

32 Robert uses the phrase 'bolster my case' in line 27 to show that he was trying to

    A change the subject.

    B end the conversation.

    C reassure Sergei.

    D correct Sergei.

33 Robert uses the example of the over-trousers to show that

    A he had been successful in getting local people to help him.

    B he had had a restricted amount of money to spend on clothes.

    C he was confident that he was well prepared for the extreme cold.

    D he had been able to negotiate good prices for his equipment.

34 What do we learn about Robert in the lecture hall?

    A He didn't want the lecturer to notice his lack of attention.

    B He was puzzled by something the lecturer had said.

    C He was unsure about what to write in the note.

    D He was apprehensive about his friend's reaction to his suggestion.

35 How can Robert's attitude to teaching best be summarised?

    A He felt it was the right career choice for him.

    B The holidays were the only positive aspect of the job.

    C He felt the job was getting too stressful.

    D He enjoyed having the respect of his students.

36 What does Robert say about Al's round-the-world trip?

    A Al never doubted that he would be successful.

    B Al tried to hide the difficulties he was facing from his friends.

    C Al was pushing himself to the limit of his capabilities.

    D Al was totally fearless as he enjoyed the adventure.

Part 6

You are going to read an article about a type of seabird, called a puffin. Six sentences have been removed from the article. Choose from the sentences **A–G** the one which fits each gap (**37–42**). There is one extra sentence which you do not need to use.

Mark your answers **on the separate answer sheet**.

Puffins in peril

*Scientist Mike Harris explains that the puffin seems about
to join the list of seabirds whose numbers are declining.*

It's a grey day in early April on the Isle of May off the east coast of Scotland. Far out to sea a small dot appears on the horizon. It rapidly increases in size, suddenly turning into a puffin that lands with a splash on the water. This bird probably hasn't seen land for five months, but now it's returning to its colony for the breeding season.

The first puffin is soon joined by others and together they bob on the sea. Newly returned birds are nervous but, as the days pass, they gain confidence and begin reclaiming the underground nesting burrows they made the previous year by tunnelling into the soft earth on the top of the cliffs. **37** They have to hurry because it takes three months to rear a chick and all the birds must leave by early August to spend time feeding intensively before the winter.

I visit the island every April, eager to see how many of the adult puffins we have caught and attached identification rings to have returned. **38** With a team of helpers I counted every occupied burrow on the island – something we undertake every five years.

The island's puffin population had been increasing every year for the previous 40 years, and so we anticipated at least 100,000 pairs. To our dismay we found just 42,000. **39** Experts from other research programmes have concluded it must be connected to where puffins spend the winter months.

Last spring we also caught and weighed some returning adults and found they were significantly lighter than the birds we caught 10 years ago. **40** Puffins are long-lived and can cope with a few poor productive seasons, but not with such a large loss of adults.

In early August, the puffin colonies empty rather abruptly. Virtually all puffins leave within a week, though a few adults remain to feed a late chick. **41** I have always believed, though, that few of them venture far from the North Sea. Now, however, the development of instruments known as geolocators, small enough to be fitted around a puffin's leg, is enabling us to test this idea.

We fitted these units to some puffins two years ago and caught the birds again last year to download the data. Some did remain within the North Sea, but others went much further. For someone who has spent years watching puffins for only part of their lives, this new technology is providing some fascinating information. **42** This would still leave us with the question of what they eat in winter and whether there are sufficient quantities of prey available.

The good news is that we now have an idea of the areas our puffins go to in winter, and we can check whether conditions there might have altered due to climate change or overfishing. Maybe we can then take some steps to help them. Hopefully it is just a local problem, because there are in fact still plenty of puffins to see around the Scottish coast.

A We weren't the only ones to wonder why this might be happening.

B From this moment on, we know remarkably little about where these birds end up and what could possibly be affecting them there.

C But we should also take into account that if a young puffin survives the winter, it will come back the following July.

D Other devices will also hopefully tell us how much time puffins spend diving for food.

E This was further evidence that something unusual is happening at sea before they return to the colony.

F Puffins are always among the earliest seabirds to lay eggs.

G Last year there was an additional task.

Part 7

You are going to read an article about the Italian painter Canaletto. For questions **43–52**, choose from the sections (**A–E**). The sections may be chosen more than once.

Mark your answers **on the separate answer sheet**.

In which section does the writer

suggest why Canaletto's work was less appreciated in his home city than elsewhere?	**43**	
give examples of how Canaletto tricks the viewer in his pictures?	**44**	
claim that Canaletto's paintings contain a kind of historical record of Venice?	**45**	
tell us where Canaletto worked on the composition of his pictures?	**46**	
mention the reason why Canaletto didn't paint exactly what he had seen?	**47**	
suggest a weakness in the work Canaletto painted away from Venice?	**48**	
give some details of Canaletto's initial painting technique?	**49**	
say that Canaletto took a risk by specialising in a particular kind of art?	**50**	
describe different artistic reactions to Venice?	**51**	
refer to the effect Canaletto's paintings had on artists in another country?	**52**	

Canaletto and Venice

An expert describes the close relationship between the great 18th century
Italian painter Canaletto and his home city.

A Canaletto's lifetime subject was the city of Venice. Apart from the works done during his decade in London, he painted virtually nothing else, and Venice has never been so minutely and extensively painted by any other artist. His response to Venice was not like the dramatic, emotional response of a visitor overpowered by the city's haunting beauty and magic, as the British painter Turner was later, for example. Canaletto's paintings, with their love of incidental detail, betray a deeper-rooted, more lasting attachment – the affection of a native Venetian.

B Canaletto depicted the city as it really was, documenting the changes in the cityscape over the years – Piazza San Marco being repaved, palaces being reconstructed, graffiti appearing and disappearing. Above all, he suffused his painting with the natural light and atmosphere of Venice which was second nature to him. When he went to London in 1746, Canaletto could not quite come to terms with painting the cooler tones and the unsympathetic climate of England, and somehow his paintings of the River Thames always ended up looking rather like the Grand Canal.

C In spite of his natural affection for Venice, Canaletto's paintings were rarely bought by his fellow Venetians. This was probably because the locals did not need reminders of their city, and also because in Venice 'view painting' was not taken very seriously in comparison with historical and religious painting, or even landscape and figure painting. To become a 'view painter' at that time was quite a brave choice and, by the end of his career, Canaletto had done much to raise the status of the genre. However, his influence was felt more among painters in England, the home of his major patrons.

D Canaletto's extraordinarily detailed and accurate scenes were perfect for the foreign tourists in Venice, who wanted souvenirs or mementoes of their visits. The more accurate the scene the better, in fact, and Canaletto's first patron, Owen McSwiney, persuaded him to change from his earlier picturesque and theatrical style to a more factual one. Instead of loose brushwork and thick paint, alongside dramatic contrasts of light and shade, Canaletto adopted more of a snapshot approach, which proved to be very commercial. His colours became brighter, the paint surface smoother, and the scenes looked more realistic. McSwiney wrote 'his excellence lies in painting things which fall immediately under his eye', as if he worked directly from nature. At a casual glance, everything in his pictures is instantly recognisable and looks exactly as it does, or did, in reality. In fact, Canaletto never painted from nature – his pictures were created in the studio.

E In working out the compositions, he used his imagination and a certain artistic licence. Although he paid the minutest attention to the detail of a decorative carving, a ship's sails or washing hanging out, Canaletto felt at liberty to distort and reorganise the main objects in his paintings in the interest of dramatic effect. He would alter the sweeping curve of the Grand Canal, for example, or include more in a composition than could be seen from any single viewpoint. The clutter of traffic on the waterways looks random and natural, but the position of each boat was carefully worked out to achieve the best effect. In this way, he conveyed the essence of Venice even if he deceived the eye. The drawings which formed the basis of his compositions range from rapid sketches of ideas for painting, done on the spot, to large-scale fully detailed preliminary drawings. Sometimes, he made precise drawings for engravers to copy, and occasionally he produced them as works of art in their own right, in which case they were finished in the studio.

WRITING (1 hour 20 minutes)

Part 1

You **must** answer this question. Write your answer in **140–190** words in an appropriate style **on the separate answer sheet**.

---

1   In your English class you have been talking about famous people. Now, your English teacher has asked you to write an essay.

Write an essay using **all** the notes and giving reasons for your point of view.

'The private lives of famous people should not be made public.' What do you think?

Notes

Write about:

1. public interest in famous people

2. famous people as role models

3. ...(your own idea)

Part 2

Write an answer to **one** of the questions **2–4** in this part. Write your answer in **140–190** words in an appropriate style **on the separate answer sheet**. Put the question number in the box at the top of the answer sheet.

---

2   You see this notice in an English-language website called Restaurant World:

> *Reviews wanted*
>
> ## A Wonderful Meal
>
> Write us a review of a restaurant where you had a wonderful meal. Tell us what the restaurant was like, describe what you ate and explain why it was so good.
>
> The best reviews will be posted on the website.

Write your **review**.

3   You see this advertisement in your local newspaper:

> **Helpers wanted**
>
> We are looking for people to work in a holiday club for English-speaking children (aged 4–8).
> Write a letter to Mr Nick Jones, the club organizer, giving details of:
> * your experience of working with children
> * your knowledge of English
> * why you would be suitable for the job.

Write your **letter of application**.

4   You see this notice in an English-language magazine:

> *Articles wanted*
>
> ## Ambition
>
> What does ambition mean to you? What ambitions do you have? How do you intend to achieve them?
>
> The best articles will be published in our magazine.

Write your **article**.

LISTENING (approximately 40 minutes)

Part 1

You will hear people talking in eight different situations.

For questions **1–8**, choose the best answer (**A**, **B** or **C**).

1   You hear two friends talking about a laptop computer.

What is the woman doing?

A persuading her friend to buy one like it

B offering to lend it to her friend for a day

C explaining why she needed a new one

2   You hear two students talking about a play they have just seen.

What do they agree was good about it?

A the script

B the set

C the actors

3   You hear two people talking about a friend.

What do they agree about him?

A He's very helpful.

B He's easy to get to know.

C He rarely complains about anything.

4   You hear a lecturer talking to some of his students about their history project.

What is he doing?

A encouraging them to ask him questions about it

B recommending some books that will help with it

C advising them on how to organise their time

5   You hear two TV sports presenters talking about their work.

What do they agree about sports presenters?

A   They're generally more effective when using a script.

B   They have to be able to relate well to their audience.

C   They should adopt an attitude that isn't too serious.

6   You hear a woman talking about a radio programme.

What does she say about the programme?

A   It provided her with a lot of useful information.

B   It was more interesting than she had expected.

C   It made her want to find out about a place.

7   You hear two music students talking about an assignment they have to do.

What are they both unsure about?

A   what to include in the piece of writing

B   how to organise the recording

C   what kind of music they should perform

8   You hear a writer talking about a book she wrote which has been turned into a film.

How does the writer feel about the film director?

A   She thinks he has made a good film.

B   She is upset because her opinion was ignored.

C   She found him easy to work with.

Part 2

You will hear a woman called Anne Ruskin giving a talk about a one-day archery course, during which she learnt to use a bow to shoot arrows at a target. For questions **9–18**, complete the sentences with a word or short phrase.

Archery

Anne used to shoot arrows from a bow made of [_____ **9**] when she was a child.

Anne only had time to read about the [_____ **10**] of archery before the beginner's archery course.

Anne's archery course took place in a [_____ **11**] .

Anne was surprised that learning to [_____ **12**] properly was so difficult.

The teacher told Anne she needed to relax her [_____ **13**] .

One of Anne's arrows went into a [_____ **14**] by accident.

During the breaks, Ann was happy to look at the [_____ **15**] and talk to other people.

Some of the people on Anne's course said that a [_____ **16**] had inspired them to try archery.

Anne was excited when the class were allowed to start [_____ **17**] .

Anne is trying to persuade her [_____ **18**] to do an archery course with her.

Part 3

You will hear five short extracts in which people are talking about when they moved their office from one building to another. For questions **19–23**, choose from the list (**A–H**) what each speaker says. Use the letters only once. There are three extra letters which you do not need to use.

A We were not allowed to do the packing ourselves.

B We decided not to blame the removal company for all the problems.

Speaker 1 [ ] **19**

C We chose certain members of staff to take responsibility for the move.

Speaker 2 [ ] **20**

Speaker 3 [ ] **21**

D We chose a removal firm with a good reputation to avoid wasting time.

Speaker 4 [ ] **22**

E We made sure our senior staff stayed with the company.

Speaker 5 [ ] **23**

F We took advantage of the move to make additional necessary changes.

G We managed not to exceed our budget.

H We expressed our concerns about the move.

Part 4

You will hear part of a radio interview with someone called Jane Brown, who is a home economist working in the food industry. For questions **24–30**, choose the best answer (**A**, **B** or **C**).

24 Why did Jane choose to study at Longley University?

    A The location suited her.

    B She knew people there.

    C The quality of the accommodation was good.

25 What did Jane like about her course?

    A She gained practical experience.

    B The teachers helped her a great deal.

    C She learned to work with other people.

26 What does Jane say about her food tasting training?

    A It was a little boring.

    B It was rather time-consuming.

    C It was sometimes stressful.

27 How did Jane feel when she was offered her first job?

    A excited to be involved in a challenging area

    B relieved to have been able to find employment

    C concerned she might not do her work well enough

28 Jane is proud that in her first job she

    A came up with her own original idea for a product.

    B proved that she was capable of working independently.

    C succeeded in doing something nobody thought she could.

29 How did working in Denmark help Jane's career?

   A She made useful contacts.

   B She came across new recipes.

   C She found a better job.

30 What aspect of her job does Jane enjoy?

   A the wide variety of activities she does

   B the opportunity to meet new people

   C the experience of trying new foods

SPEAKING (14 minutes)

You take the Speaking test with another candidate (possibly two candidates), referred to here as your partner. There are two examiners. One will speak to you and your partner and the other will be listening. Both examiners will award marks.

Part 1 (2 minutes)

The examiner asks you and your partner questions about yourselves. You may be asked about things like 'your home town', 'your interests', 'your career plans', etc.

Part 2 (a one-minute 'long turn' for each candidate, plus a 30-second response from the second candidate)

The examiner gives you two photographs and asks you to talk about them for one minute. The examiner then asks your partner a question about your photographs and your partner responds briefly.

Then the examiner gives your partner two different photographs. Your partner talks about these photographs for one minute. This time the examiner asks you a question about your partner's photographs and you respond briefly.

Part 3 (4 minutes)

The examiner asks you and your partner to talk together. They give you a task to look at so you can think about and discuss an idea, giving reasons for your opinion. For example, you may be asked to think about some changes in the world, or about spending free time with your family. After you have discussed the task for about two minutes with your partner, the examiner will ask you a follow-up question, which you should discuss for a further minute.

Part 4 (4 minutes)

The examiner asks some further questions, which leads to a more general discussion of what you have talked about in Part 3. You may comment on your partner's answers if you wish.

Test 8

READING AND USE OF ENGLISH (1 hour 15 minutes)

Part 1

For questions **1–8**, read the text below and decide which answer (**A**, **B**, **C** or **D**) best fits each gap. There is an example at the beginning (**0**).

Mark your answers **on the separate answer sheet**.

Example:

0 **A** late   **B** previous   **C** closing   **D** final

0	A	B	C	D
	▬	▭	▭	▭

Dr Joseph Bell

Dr Joseph Bell was a distinguished Scottish doctor and professor at Edinburgh University in the **(0)** .... nineteenth century. He had remarkable powers of observation and deduction. This **(1)** .... him to accumulate useful information about patients in a very **(2)** .... space of time.

He was very good at **(3)** .... where his patients were from by identifying small differences in their accents. He could also **(4)** .... a patient's occupation from marks on their hand. He claimed to be able to **(5)** .... a sailor from a soldier just from the way they moved. If he identified a person as a sailor he would look for any tattoos that might assist him in knowing where their travels had **(6)** .... them.

Dr Bell's skills for observation and deduction **(7)** .... a great impression on his students, particularly on one called Arthur Conan Doyle. Conan Doyle went on to create the famous fictional detective Sherlock Holmes, whose character was **(8)** .... on that of Dr Bell.

1   **A**   enabled   **B**   authorised   **C**   guaranteed   **D**   caused

2   **A**   small   **B**   rapid   **C**   narrow   **D**   short

3   **A**   showing off   **B**   working out   **C**   setting down   **D**   turning up

4   **A**   relate   **B**   acknowledge   **C**   solve   **D**   determine

5   **A**   change   **B**   differ   **C**   distinguish   **D**   contrast

6   **A**   transported   **B**   brought   **C**   conveyed   **D**   taken

7   **A**   set   **B**   made   **C**   formed   **D**   put

8   **A**   applied   **B**   established   **C**   based   **D**   written

Part 2

For questions **9–16**, read the text below and think of the word which best fits each gap. Use only **one** word in each gap. There is an example at the beginning (**0**).

Write your answers **IN CAPITAL LETTERS on the separate answer sheet**.

Example: | 0 | | A | R | E | | | | | | | | | | | | | | | |

The importance of laughter

Psychologists tell us that humour and laughter **(0)** .... good for our social relationships. Having a good sense of humour is often regarded **(9)** .... being one of the most important characteristics that people look **(10)** .... in a friend. In classrooms, a humorous teacher can make learning far **(11)** .... enjoyable and improve a student's motivation.

In one study, students on a psychology course **(12)** .... split into two different groups: one group was taught with a certain amount of humour, and the other with **(13)** .... humour at all. Later, when researchers tested the students to see how much they had retained of **(14)** .... they had heard in the lectures, they found that those **(15)** .... had attended lectures containing humour scored significantly higher than the other students.

Humour and laughter make us feel happy, and our laughter makes others laugh as **(16)** .... , so if we laugh a lot we may be helping to make other people feel happy.

Part 3

For questions **17–24**, read the text below. Use the word given in capitals at the end of some of the lines to form a word that fits in the gap **in the same line**. There is an example at the beginning **(0)**.

Write your answers **IN CAPITAL LETTERS on the separate answer sheet.**

Example: | 0 | F | A | S | C | I | N | A | T | I | O | N | | | | | | | |

A man happy in his work

Flying has always had a **(0)** .... for me. During my childhood I was often taken to air shows, where I could see planes close up and even go inside them. However, it was not until I was twenty that I made the **(17)** .... to apply for an eighteen-month training course to become a pilot. There was no funding available for students on this course so **(18)** .... I had to wait six months for a suitable job **(19)** .... , but then the **(20)** .... I had shown was rewarded when I got a job with a large airline.

I've been a pilot for three years now, and I remain just as **(21)** .... about flying. I love the modern jet aircraft with all their sophisticated equipment as well as the **(22)** .... of challenges that occur on a **(23)** .... basis. And, of course, it's wonderful to visit places all over the world, not to mention the **(24)** .... views I get when I'm flying.

FASCINATE

DECIDE

FORTUNATE
VACANT
COMMIT

ENTHUSIASM

VARY
DAY
SPECTACLE

Part 4

For questions **25–30**, complete the second sentence so that it has a similar meaning to the first sentence, using the word given. **Do not change the word given**. You must use between **two** and **five** words, including the word given. Here is an example (**0**).

Example:

0   A very friendly taxi driver drove us into town.

   DRIVEN

   We .... a very friendly taxi driver.

The gap can be filled by the words 'were driven into town by', so you write:

Example:	0	*WERE DRIVEN INTO TOWN BY*

Write **only** the missing words **IN CAPITAL LETTERS on the separate answer sheet**.

---

25   Tom was so tired that he did not even get undressed before he lay down on his bed.

   TAKE

   Tom was so tired that he did not even .... before he lay down on his bed.

26   It was Samantha's responsibility to ring all the members of the team.

   RESPONSIBLE

   Samantha .... all the members of the team.

27   I had expected to enjoy the film more than I did.

   AS

   The film was .... I had expected.

28 Helen finally managed to think of a solution to her problem.

COMING

Helen finally succeeded .... a solution to her problem.

29 My sister regrets buying a second-hand car.

WISHES

My sister .... a second-hand car.

30 I was late for work because I missed my bus.

ACCOUNT

I was late for work .... my bus.

Part 5

You are going to read a newspaper article about a polar explorer. For questions **31–36**, choose the answer (**A**, **B**, **C** or **D**) which you think fits best according to the text.

Mark your answers **on the separate answer sheet**.

Pen Hadow – polar explorer

The explorer is risking his life in the Arctic again,
this time for all of us. Cole Moretonin reports.

In 2004, Pen Hadow became the first person to trek to the North Pole alone, without being resupplied on the way. That meant swimming through unimaginably cold waters, fighting frostbite and risking encounters with polar bears. Just eight months later, he made a similar trip to the South Pole. Now he is back in the Arctic again, preparing for an expedition he says is even more ambitious. Explorers are confident, driven individuals. They have to be. This time, however, there is far more at stake. Pen and two colleagues will set out on a three-month, 1,000-kilometre trek to the North Pole, taking detailed measurements of the thickness and density of the ice. Nobody has ever done this before, and he knows the results will be of vital importance to the scientific community. This will be the truest picture yet of what global warming is doing to the ice that covers the polar region.

Pen is married to Mary, a horsewoman, who says he has a 'spine of steel' and who shares his love of the outdoors. She helps to run his polar guide business and claims to be more worried about him when he's at home: 'He's in more danger driving along the motorway because I know that in his head he's somewhere in the Arctic.' For fun, she once competed against him in a famous mountain event in which riders on horseback race against people on foot. Mary and her horse finished an hour ahead of Pen.

Pen and Mary live in the country with their two children. 'It's much harder to be away from them this time,' he admits. 'They were one and five when I last went, and I made a mistake in the way I said goodbye. I thought it would be a good idea to say to my son, "You're the man of the house now, look after your mum

and your sister." He absolutely took it to heart, asking his mum how she was all the time, but the strain eventually became too much. While it was well intentioned, it was an unfair thing to do.' For similar reasons he is planning to have very little contact with them while in the Arctic. 'If you call them, you remind them how far away you are.'

line 40

He is spending these last days before departure preparing his kit, obsessively. 'Out on the ice, one is virtually incapable of mending things or doing anything that isn't absolutely straightforward,' he says. With him will be Ann Daniels, one of the world's leading polar explorers, and the expedition photographer, Martin Hartley. They will be supported by a crew of six, flying in supplies. Being part of a team is actually more stressful to someone with his mentality, says Pen, and something else is on his mind too. 'I'm going to be 47 on Thursday. I've done far less training than I'm comfortable with.' Why? 'Organisational things always seem more urgent. So I'm almost fearful of what I'm going to ask of myself.'

Pen believes his mission reconnects exploration with the search for knowledge that drove previous generations into the unknown. 'Making it to the North Pole was ultimately a personal ambition,' he admits, 'and of limited value to anyone beyond the polar adventuring community. This time, scientists will profit from the data, and we're creating a platform in which to engage as many people as possible in what's happening in the Arctic Ocean. This is important work, and nobody can do it but us,' he says. 'Our skills, which are otherwise bizarre and socially redundant, have become hyper-relevant. Suddenly, we're socially useful again.'

31 In the first paragraph, what do we learn about Pen Hadow's opinion of the new expedition?

   A He feels certain that it will be successful.
   B He thinks it may be harder than his previous journeys.
   C He is aware of the huge significance of its aims.
   D He is looking forward to the scientific work it will involve.

32 What does Mary Hadow think about her husband?

   A He isn't as determined as she is.
   B He can't run as quickly as he thinks he can.
   C He hasn't got enough time to manage his business properly.
   D He finds it hard to think about anything except his expeditions.

33 When talking about leaving his children for long periods, Pen mentions feeling

   A ashamed that his wife has had to look after them so much.
   B guilty that he once added to the pressure caused by his absence.
   C sad that he is missing so much of their growing up.
   D sorry that he can't telephone more often.

34 What does 'took it to heart' mean in line 40?

   A He memorised his father's words.
   B He carried out his father's words precisely.
   C He started to feel unwell.
   D He was afraid of the responsibility.

35 What is worrying Pen about the new expedition?

   A whether he will still be fit enough to take part
   B whether he will be mentally prepared
   C whether the equipment will work properly in icy conditions
   D whether the arrangements he has made will turn out well

36 When he compares the new expedition to his previous ones, Pen feels

   A pleased that more people will benefit from it.
   B uncertain if it will collect information.
   C doubtful about its long-term usefulness.
   D relieved that the general public will be more supportive.

Part 6

You are going to read an article about the sport of inline skating. Six sentences have been removed from the text. Choose from the sentences **A–G** the one which fits each gap (**37–42**). There is one extra sentence which you do not need to use.

Mark your answers **on the separate answer sheet**.

Inline Skating

The popularity of inline skating is growing all the time.

No doubt about it, inline skating is one of the world's most popular street sports. Different people call it different things. Rollerblade was the original American skate manufacturer and that's why many call it rollerblading. Others shorten this to blading, while still others prefer inline skating (because the wheels on each skate are in line).

37 Inline skating has taken the concept of self-propelled wheels into a new dimension which allows skaters of the most basic ability to move with grace, speed and style, and feel good about doing it. A huge attraction is that you can do it anywhere where there is a smooth, hard surface and if you're really keen, you can even do it off-road too.

But the very popularity of the sport everywhere has created something of a problem. The 'Ban all Skaters' group, made up of opponents of the sport, has never been far behind. **38** No matter – people will keep on skating wherever they can.

So the difficulty lies in changing the attitude of established local authorities, which are so often dominated by older people who have no concept of the joy of inline skating, don't want anything to do with it, and simply dismiss the sport as a branch of the current youth culture they can do without.

We know they are wrong. **39** It is a sport which offers everyone a brilliant way to get up off the couch, whizz around outside, have fun, get fit, get involved, develop skills and learn team-work.

In time, all skaters will be allowed to go about their business and co-exist in harmony with other users of tarmac. **40** So skaters should take care not to adopt a selfish attitude to others, because annoying other people might eventually lead to a situation where the skaters' own enjoyment or freedom of movement is curtailed.

Kids as young as five or six can learn to skate well. **41** And in between those two extremes skating is no less important as a way for those in their teen years to avoid the trap of urban boredom, which can create problems in contemporary society.

To qualify as an inline skater, you just have to get through the basics of pushing off, turning and stopping – all easy techniques which most people can learn to handle in half a dozen sessions. **42** Next you can learn to skate faster, turn tighter, stop faster, skate through slalom cones (just use tin cans) forwards and maybe backwards. Then you can learn how to go up and down hills and perhaps some clever tricks as well.

A Inline skating is not just about kids whose wishes can be ignored.

B Once up and running, it's all about consolidating what's been learned, enjoying the feel of your wheels and getting better.

C They all add up to the great new world of inlining.

D What's more, with all the right padding and protection, adults can start to skate safely at an age when they are collecting their pensions.

E In some areas it has been successful in implementing notorious and strict skating prohibitions, such as the closure of most of London's parks to skaters.

F The name doesn't really matter; it's the impact it has had that is important.

G Indeed, it's all about the right to enjoy life's little – and not so little – pleasures.

Part 7

You are going to read an article about a psychology test carried out on very young children. For questions **43–52**, choose from the sections (**A–D**). The sections may be chosen more than once.

Mark your answers **on the separate answer sheet**.

In which section does the writer mention

how a child's background can affect behaviour?	43
that the results of Mischel's long-term research were surprising?	44
reasons for questioning the results of the original experiment?	45
claims that training young children to resist temptation will have long-term benefits?	46
the proportion of very young children who were able to resist temptation?	47
an everyday example of the need for self-control?	48
that Mischel may have oversimplified the route to success in life?	49
that Mischel's own life experience has influenced his work?	50
strategies employed by participants during the test procedure?	51
two major factors which affect everyone's ability to resist temptation?	52

The Marshmallow Test

A psychology experiment carried out with a group of pre-school children in California in 1968 led to the development of ideas that are still relevant today.

A

In 1968, Walter Mischel set a challenge for a group of children aged three to five at the nursery school his daughters attended in California. A researcher offered each of them a marshmallow and then left them alone in the room. If they could resist eating the colourful sweet until the researcher returned up to 15 minutes later, they would be given a second sweet. Some children ate the marshmallow straight away, but most would engage in unintentionally comic attempts to resist temptation. They looked all around the room to avoid seeing the sweet, covered their eyes, wiggled around in their seats or sang to themselves. They pulled funny faces, played with their hair, picked up the marshmallow and just pretended to take a bite. They sniffed it, pushed it away from them or covered it up. If two children were doing the experiment together, they engaged in a conversation about how they could work together to reach the goal of doubling their pleasure. About a third of the children, the researchers reported, managed to wait long enough to get the second treat.

B

What Mischel, a clinical psychologist, wanted was to understand how children learned to deal with temptation. Over the following years, the group of children remained friends. When Mischel chatted to his daughters about their former classmates, he began to notice an interesting pattern: the children who had exhibited the most restraint in the 'marshmallow test' were doing better in life than their peers. He decided to investigate further. For more than 40 years, Mischel followed the lives of the nursery students. His findings were extraordinary. It turns out that being able to resist a treat at the age of five is a strong predictor of success in life: you are more likely to perform well at school and develop self-confidence and less likely to become obese, develop addictions or get divorced.

C

Mischel still teaches psychology at Columbia University and has just written *The Marshmallow Test*, a book summing up half a century of research. When Mischel was young, his family was forced to move from a comfortable life in Austria to the US. They settled in Brooklyn, where they opened a bargain shopping store. Business was never good and Mischel believes that moving from 'upper middle class to extreme poverty' shaped his outlook. He is concerned with trying to reduce the impact of deprivation on an individual's life chances. The conclusion he draws from his marshmallow research is positive: some people may be naturally disciplined but the ability to resist temptation is a skill that can also be taught. Teach children self-control early and you can improve their prospects.

D

However, no single characteristic – such as self-control – can explain success or failure. Some critics have pointed out that Mischel's original subjects were themselves children of university professors and graduate students – not exactly a representative sample. Other scientists noted that variations in home environment could account for differences: stable homes and one-child families encourage self-control, whereas in less stable homes and those with many children, if you don't grab a marshmallow now there won't be any left in 15 minutes. Mischel answers these critics by noting that studies in a wide variety of schools found similar results. He acknowledges that the environment shapes our ability to resist temptation and observes that genetics plays a role too. But he still believes that the ability to resist temptation can be learnt and encouraged. I asked Mischel whether self-control comes easily to him. 'Not at all,' he said. 'I have great difficulties in waiting. It's still difficult for me to wait in a queue in the bank.'

WRITING (1 hour 20 minutes)

Part 1

You **must** answer this question. Write your answer in **140–190** words in an appropriate style **on the separate answer sheet**.

---

1 In your English class you have been talking about learning history at school. Now, your English teacher has asked you to write an essay.

Write an essay using **all** the notes and giving reasons for your point of view.

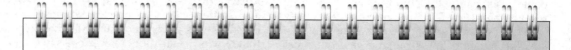

'Everyone should be taught the history of their own country.' Do you agree?

Notes

Write about:

1. what people can learn from the past

2. it's more important to think about the future

3. ...(your own idea)

Part 2

Write an answer to **one** of the questions **2–4** in this part. Write your answer in **140–190** words in an appropriate style **on the separate answer sheet**. Put the question number in the box at the top of the answer sheet.

2   Your English teacher has asked you to write a report on transport facilities in your area.
    In your report, you should:

- describe the existing transport facilities
- explain what's good and bad about them
- suggest how they could be improved in the future.

Write your **report**.

3   You have received this email from your English-speaking friend, Susan:

> **From: Susan**
> **Subject: Money!**
>
> Hi!
> I've just won £1,000 in a photography competition. I could spend it all on a fantastic holiday or I could put it in my bank account, or I could give it to my parents who don't have much money.
> What do you suggest I do?
> Thanks,
> Susan

Write your **email**.

4   You see this in an English-language magazine.

> *Articles wanted*
>
> ## Being kind
>
> What does being kind mean to you?
>
> Why is it important to be kind?
>
> We will publish the best articles in the next magazine.

Write your **article**.

LISTENING (approximately 40 minutes)

Part 1

You will hear people talking in eight different situations.

For questions **1–8**, choose the best answer (**A**, **B** or **C**).

1   You hear two people talking about some music they're listening to.

What does the man say about the song?

A It cheers him up.

B It reminds him of his family.

C It inspired him to take up a musical instrument.

2   You hear part of a radio programme in which a teacher is talking about her own education.

Why did she become a teacher?

A She enjoyed her own time at school very much.

B She was encouraged to do so by colleagues.

C She wanted others to have the same opportunities as her.

3   You hear a woman telling a friend about a new job she has.

What problem does she have with the job?

A being asked to do tasks she's not suited for

B being too busy at certain times of day

C being disrespected by some customers

4   You hear two students talking about an architecture course.

What do they agree about?

A There is too much work on the course.

B Their fellow students are creative people.

C The course is taught in an interesting way.

5   You hear two students talking about the chemistry laboratories at their college.

What does the woman say about the laboratories?

A The equipment in them should be updated.

B They are not large enough.

C They need redecorating.

6   You hear a woman talking about a place she used to visit as a child.

What point is she making?

A She might be disappointed if she returned there.

B She prefers more sophisticated holidays now.

C The place appeals more to children than adults.

7   You hear a runner telling his friend about a sports injury he has.

What did his doctor advise?

A keep going with some training

B introduce other sports very gradually

C start running very slowly

8   You hear a woman talking about her favourite radio programme.

What does she say about the stories in the programme?

A The creative element in them is what makes them work.

B They tend to vary in how interesting they are.

C They contain messages we can all learn from.

Part 2

You will hear a man called Peter Green talking about a group expedition he went on to the South Pole for a TV documentary. For questions **9–18**, complete the sentences with a word or short phrase.

Expedition to South Pole

Peter was working as an [_____ **9**] when he applied to join the expedition.

On the expedition, Peter and his group went to the South Pole on [_____ **10**] instead of more typical means of transport.

Peter says that his greatest challenge was the [_____ **11**] he suffered.

Peter says that ensuring they could get enough [_____ **12**] took up a good deal of the group's time.

Peter was surprised at how quickly his [_____ **13**] decreased.

Peter's [_____ **14**] were affected by the cold during the expedition.

One of Peter's teammates had a chest infection and the lack of [_____ **15**] made it worse.

When they reached the [_____ **16**] point, Peter's team were given a medical check.

Peter felt a great sense of [_____ **17**] when he reached the pole.

Peter uses the word [_____ **18**] to describe the environment at the South Pole.

Part 3

You will hear five short extracts in which people are talking about how to give good presentations. For questions **19–23**, choose from the list (**A–H**) what advice each person gives. Use the letters only once. There are three extra letters which you do not need to use.

A   Keep your presentation short.

B   Remember to repeat your main point.

Speaker 1 | 19 |

C   Support your presentation with visuals.

Speaker 2 | 20 |

D   Add some humour.

Speaker 3 | 21 |

E   Practise giving your presentation.

Speaker 4 | 22 |

F   Try to relax during your presentation.

Speaker 5 | 23 |

G   Don't try to memorise every word.

H   Find out about your audience.

Part 4

You will hear an interview with a woman called Maggie Wharton who is skilled in the sport of kitesurfing. For questions **24–30**, choose the best answer (**A**, **B** or **C**).

24 Maggie says it took her a long time to learn to kitesurf because

    A the equipment wasn't widely available.

    B it was hard to find the right assistance.

    C she needed to build up her strength.

25 In Maggie's opinion, since she began kitesurfing

    A suitable locations have been more clearly identified.

    B attitudes to some aspects of safety have changed.

    C participants have become better informed about sea conditions.

26 Maggie hopes that by competing in Fiji, she will

    A encourage others to take up the sport.

    B have the chance to pick up some new moves.

    C be invited to start organising future events.

27 During one distance event, Maggie became slightly worried when

    A she had to switch to different equipment.

    B she experienced a great deal of pain.

    C she lost sight of the people helping her.

28 Maggie thinks her success is due to the fact that

   A the sport suits her character very well.

   B her family have given her a lot of support.

   C she has the opportunity to practise regularly.

29 Maggie says that some new kitesurfers she's met

   A are likely to develop the sport in interesting ways.

   B are unwilling to focus on basic techniques first of all.

   C are too worried about the rules of the sport.

30 What does Maggie hope to do in the future?

   A find sources of investment for her sport

   B continue to compete at a high level

   C set up a kitesurfing school

SPEAKING (14 minutes)

You take the Speaking test with another candidate (possibly two candidates), referred to here as your partner. There are two examiners. One will speak to you and your partner and the other will be listening. Both examiners will award marks.

Part 1 (2 minutes)

The examiner asks you and your partner questions about yourselves. You may be asked about things like 'your home town', 'your interests', 'your career plans', etc.

Part 2 (a one-minute 'long turn' for each candidate, plus a 30-second response from the second candidate)

The examiner gives you two photographs and asks you to talk about them for one minute. The examiner then asks your partner a question about your photographs and your partner responds briefly.

Then the examiner gives your partner two different photographs. Your partner talks about these photographs for one minute. This time the examiner asks you a question about your partner's photographs and you respond briefly.

Part 3 (4 minutes)

The examiner asks you and your partner to talk together. They give you a task to look at so you can think about and discuss an idea, giving reasons for your opinion. For example, you may be asked to think about some changes in the world, or about spending free time with your family. After you have discussed the task for about two minutes with your partner, the examiner will ask you a follow-up question, which you should discuss for a further minute.

Part 4 (4 minutes)

The examiner asks some further questions, which leads to a more general discussion of what you have talked about in Part 3. You may comment on your partner's answers if you wish.

Frames for the Speaking test

Test 5

Note: In the examination, there will be both an assessor and an interlocutor in the room. The visual material for **Test 5** appears on pages C1 and C2 (Part 2), and C3 (Part 3).

Part 1　2 minutes (3 minutes for groups of three)

Interlocutor:　Good morning/afternoon/evening. My name is .... and this is my colleague ....
And your names are?
Can I have your mark sheets, please?
Thank you.

- Where are you from, *(Candidate A)*?
- And you, *(Candidate B)*?

First, we'd like to know something about you.

Select one or more questions from any of the following categories, as appropriate.

Travel
- Do you enjoy long journeys? (What do you do to pass the time?)
- Do you have to travel far every day? (Where do you have to go?)
- Do you prefer to travel by car or public transport? (Why?)
- Tell us about an interesting place you've travelled to.

Study or work
- What good memories do you have of school?
- Is there anything you would like to study in the future? (Why?)
- Have you ever had a part-time job? (What do/did you do? Do/Did you enjoy it?)
- Would you prefer to work for a big or small company? (Why?)

Sports and hobbies
- Do you prefer individual sports or team sports? (Why?)
- Which is the most popular sport in your country? (Why do you think it's popular?)
- How much time do you spend listening to music? (What kind of music do you like?)
- Do you enjoy playing computer games in your free time? (Why? / Why not?)

Part 2   4 minutes (6 minutes for groups of three)

Guided tours
Doing exercise

Interlocutor:	In this part of the test, I'm going to give each of you two photographs. I'd like you to talk about your photographs on your own for about a minute, and also to answer a question about your partner's photographs.
	(Candidate A), it's your turn first. Here are your photographs. They show people going on different guided tours.
	Indicate the pictures on page C1 to the candidates.
	I'd like you to compare the photographs, and say what you think the people are enjoying about these guided tours.
	All right?
Candidate A:	*[1 minute.]*
Interlocutor:	Thank you.
	(Candidate B), would you like to visit either of these places? ...... (Why? / Why not?)
Candidate B:	*[Approximately 30 seconds.]*
Interlocutor:	Thank you.
	Now, *(Candidate B)*, here are your photographs. They show people doing exercise in different ways.
	Indicate the pictures on page C2 to the candidates.
	I'd like you to compare the photographs, and say why the people have decided to exercise in these ways.
	All right?
Candidate B:	*[1 minute.]*
Interlocutor:	Thank you.
	(Candidate A), which of these things would you prefer to do? ...... (Why?)
Candidate A:	*[Approximately 30 seconds.]*
Interlocutor:	Thank you.

Parts 3 and 4   8 minutes (11 minutes for groups of three)

Part 3

Keeping up to date

Interlocutor:	Now, I'd like you to talk about something together for about two minutes *(3 minutes for groups of three)*.
	Many people say that it's important to keep up to date with all the changes in the world. Here are some things in the world that often change to think about and a question for you to discuss. First you have some time to look at the task.
	Indicate the text on page C3 to the candidates. Allow 15 seconds.
	Now, talk to each other about which two things you think it's most important to keep up to date with.
Candidates:	*[2 minutes (3 minutes for groups of three).]*
Interlocutor:	Thank you. Now you have about a minute to decide what you think is the biggest advantage of keeping up to date with all the changes in the world.
Candidates:	*[1 minute (for pairs and groups of three).]*
Interlocutor:	Thank you.

Part 4

Interlocutor: *Use the following questions, in order, as appropriate:*

- Some people say that we spend too much time checking for updates on social networking websites. Do you agree? (Why? / Why not?)

> *Select any of the following prompts, as appropriate:*
> - What do you think?
> - Do you agree?
> - And you?

- Do you think the best way to keep up to date with changes in the world is to watch television? (Why? / Why not?)

- Some people say the world is changing so fast that we can't keep up to date with everything. Do you agree? (Why? / Why not?)

- How important is it for people to have change in their lives?

- Some people don't like it when things change. Why do you think that is?

- Do you think people these days are only interested in new things and ignore history and tradition? (Why? / Why not?)

Thank you. That is the end of the test.

Test 6

Note: In the examination, there will be both an assessor and an interlocutor in the room.
The visual material for **Test 6** appears on pages C4 and C5 (Part 2), and C6 (Part 3).

Part 1   2 minutes (3 minutes for groups of three)

Interlocutor: Good morning/afternoon/evening. My name is .... and this is
my colleague ....
And your names are?
Can I have your mark sheets, please?
Thank you.

* Where are you from, *(Candidate A)*?
* And you, *(Candidate B)*?

First, we'd like to know something about you.

Select one or more questions from any of the following categories,
as appropriate.

Travel
* Do you enjoy long journeys? (What do you do to pass the time?)
* Do you have to travel far every day? (Where do you have to go?)
* Do you prefer to travel by car or public transport? (Why?)
* Tell us about an interesting place you've travelled to.

Study or work
* What good memories do you have of school?
* Is there anything you would like to study in the future? (Why?)
* Have you ever had a part-time job? (What do/did you do?
  Do/Did you enjoy it?)
* Would you prefer to work for a big or small company? (Why?)

Sports and hobbies
* Do you prefer individual sports or team sports? (Why?)
* Which is the most popular sport in your country? (Why do you
  think it's popular?)
* How much time do you spend listening to music? (What kind of
  music do you like?)
* Do you enjoy playing computer games in your free time? (Why? /
  Why not?)

Part 2   4 minutes (6 minutes for groups of three)

Giving advice
Looking at beautiful things

Interlocutor:	In this part of the test, I'm going to give each of you two photographs. I'd like you to talk about your photographs on your own for about a minute, and also to answer a question about your partner's photographs.
	(Candidate A), it's your turn first. Here are your photographs. They show people giving advice in different situations.
	Indicate the pictures on page C4 to the candidates.
	I'd like you to compare the photographs, and say why it might be important to give advice in these situations.
	All right?
Candidate A:	*[1 minute.]*
Interlocutor:	Thank you.
	(Candidate B), do you like listening to advice? ...... (Why? / Why not?)
Candidate B:	*[Approximately 30 seconds.]*
Interlocutor:	Thank you.
	Now, *(Candidate B)*, here are your photographs. They show people looking at beautiful things.
	Indicate the pictures on page C5 to the candidates.
	I'd like you to compare the photographs, and say why you think these people are looking at these beautiful things.
	All right?
Candidate B:	*[1 minute.]*
Interlocutor:	Thank you.
	(Candidate A), do you enjoy going to museums and galleries? ...... (Why? / Why not?)
Candidate A:	*[Approximately 30 seconds.]*
Interlocutor:	Thank you.

Parts 3 and 4   8 minutes (11 minutes for groups of three)

Part 3
Boredom

Interlocutor:	Now, I'd like you to talk about something together for about two minutes *(3 minutes for groups of three)*.
	Here are some reasons why it might be a good idea for people to change the way they spend their free time. First you have some time to look at the task.
	Indicate the text on page C6 to the candidates. Allow 15 seconds.
	Now, talk to each other about why people should change the way they spend their free time.
Candidates:	*[2 minutes (3 minutes for groups of three).]*
Interlocutor:	Thank you. Now you have about a minute to decide which is the most important reason for changing the way we spend our free time.
Candidates:	*[1 minute (for pairs and groups of three).]*
Interlocutor:	Thank you.

Part 4

Interlocutor: *Use the following questions, in order, as appropriate:*

- Should schools and colleges organise free time activities for students at weekends? (Why? / Why not?)

- Do you think it's true that you will always enjoy yourself if you're with other people? (Why? / Why not?)

Select any of the following prompts, as appropriate:

- What do you think?
- Do you agree?
- And you?

- Some people say that it's important to entertain yourself rather than expect other people to do it all the time. What do you think?

- Is it a good idea to have a lot of different interests or just one or two? (Why? / Why not?)

- Do you think it's important to be busy all the time? (Why? / Why not?)

- Some people say we don't have enough free time these days. What do you think?

Thank you. That is the end of the test.

Test 7

Note: In the examination, there will be both an assessor and an interlocutor in the room.
  The visual material for **Test 7** appears on pages C7 and C8 (Part 2), and C9 (Part 3).

Part 1   2 minutes (3 minutes for groups of three)

Interlocutor:

Good morning/afternoon/evening. My name is .... and this is my colleague ....
And your names are?
Can I have your mark sheets, please?
Thank you.

- Where are you from, *(Candidate A)*?
- And you, *(Candidate B)*?

First we'd like to know something about you.

Select one or more questions from any of the following categories, as appropriate.

Travel
- Do you enjoy long journeys? (What do you do to pass the time?)
- Do you have to travel far every day? (Where do you have to go?)
- Do you prefer to travel by car or public transport? (Why?)
- Tell us about an interesting place you've travelled to.

Study or work
- What good memories do you have of school?
- Is there anything you would like to study in the future? (Why?)
- Have you ever had a part-time job? (What do/did you do? Do/Did you enjoy it?)
- Would you prefer to work for a big or small company? (Why?)

Sports and hobbies
- Do you prefer individual sports or team sports? (Why?)
- Which is the most popular sport in your country? (Why do you think it's popular?)
- How much time do you spend listening to music? (What kind of music do you like?)
- Do you enjoy playing computer games in your free time? (Why? / Why not?)

Part 2   4 minutes (6 minutes for groups of three)

Quiet places
At night

Interlocutor:	In this part of the test, I'm going to give each of you two photographs. I'd like you to talk about your photographs on your own for about a minute, and also to answer a question about your partner's photographs.
	(Candidate A), it's your turn first. Here are your photographs. They show people spending time in quiet places.
	Indicate the pictures on page C7 to the candidates.
	I'd like you to compare the photographs, and say why you think the people have decided to spend time in these quiet places.
	All right?
Candidate A:	*[1 minute.]*
Interlocutor:	Thank you.
	(Candidate B), which of these places would you prefer to spend time in? ...... (Why?)
Candidate B:	*[Approximately 30 seconds.]*
Interlocutor:	Thank you.
	Now, *(Candidate B)*, here are your photographs. They show people doing different things at night.
	Indicate the pictures on page C8 to the candidates.
	I'd like you to compare the photographs, and say what you think the people might be enjoying about doing these things at night.
	All right?
Candidate B:	*[1 minute.]*
Interlocutor:	Thank you.
	(Candidate A), which of these things would you prefer to do? ..... (Why?)
Candidate A:	*[Approximately 30 seconds.]*
Interlocutor:	Thank you.

Parts 3 and 4   8 minutes (11 minutes for groups of three)

Part 3

Other cultures

Interlocutor:	Now, I'd like you to talk about something together for about two minutes *(3 minutes for groups of three)*.
	Many people say that it's important to learn about other cultures and their customs. Here are some reasons for this and a question for you to discuss. First you have some time to look at the task.
	Indicate the text on page C9 to the candidates. Allow 15 seconds.
	Now, talk to each other about whether it's important to learn about other cultures and their customs.
Candidates:	*[2 minutes (3 minutes for groups of three).]*
Interlocutor:	Thank you. Now you have about a minute to decide which is the most important reason for learning about other cultures.
Candidates:	*[1 minute (for pairs and groups of three).]*
Interlocutor:	Thank you.

Part 4

Interlocutor: *Use the following questions, in order, as appropriate:*

- Are you interested in the cultures of other countries, for example their music or food? (Why? / Why not?)

- Can we learn a lot about the culture of a country when we're on holiday there? (Why? / Why not?)

> *Select any of the following prompts, as appropriate:*
>
> - What do you think?
> - Do you agree?
> - And you?

- Should students spend more time learning about other cultures when they are at school? (Why? / Why not?)

- Some students have the opportunity to study in another country. Is this a good thing to do? (Why? / Why not?)

- Do you think it's true that the internet has helped us understand people in other countries? (Why? / Why not?)

- Some people say that these days that there aren't many big cultural differences between countries. Do you agree? (Why? / Why not?)

Thank you. That is the end of the test.

Test 8

Note: In the examination, there will be both an assessor and an interlocutor in the room.
  The visual material for **Test 8** appears on pages C10 and C11 (Part 2), and C12 (Part 3).

Part 1   2 minutes (3 minutes for groups of three)

Interlocutor: Good morning/afternoon/evening. My name is .... and this is
                 my colleague ....
                 And your names are?
                 Can I have your mark sheets, please?
                 Thank you.

- Where are you from, *(Candidate A)*?
- And you, *(Candidate B)*?

First we'd like to know something about you.

*Select one or more questions from any of the following categories,
as appropriate.*

Travel
- Do you enjoy long journeys? (What do you do to pass the time?)
- Do you have to travel far every day? (Where do you have to go?)
- Do you prefer to travel by car or public transport? (Why?)
- Tell us about an interesting place you've travelled to.

Study or work
- What good memories do you have of school?
- Is there anything you would like to study in the future? (Why?)
- Have you ever had a part-time job? (What do/did you do?
  Do/Did you enjoy it?)
- Would you prefer to work for a big or small company? (Why?)

Sports and hobbies
- Do you prefer individual sports or team sports? (Why?)
- Which is the most popular sport in your country? (Why do you
  think it's popular?)
- How much time do you spend listening to music? (What kind of
  music do you like?)
- Do you enjoy playing computer games in your free time? (Why? /
  Why not?)

Part 2   4 minutes (6 minutes for groups of three)

By the river
Attending big events

Interlocutor:	In this part of the test, I'm going to give each of you two photographs. I'd like you to talk about your photographs on your own for about a minute, and also to answer a question about your partner's photographs.
	(Candidate A), it's your turn first. Here are your photographs. They show people spending time by different rivers.
	Indicate the pictures on page C10 to the candidates.
	I'd like you to compare the photographs, and say what you think the people are enjoying about spending time by the different rivers.
	All right?
Candidate A:	*[1 minute.]*
Interlocutor:	Thank you.
	(Candidate B), which of these things would you prefer to do? ...... (Why?)
Candidate B:	*[Approximately 30 seconds.]*
Interlocutor:	Thank you.
	Now, *(Candidate B)*, here are your photographs. They show people at different big events.
	Indicate the pictures on page C11 to the candidates.
	I'd like you to compare the photographs, and say what you think the people are enjoying about being at these events.
	All right?
Candidate B:	*[1 minute.]*
Interlocutor:	Thank you.
	(Candidate A), which of these events would you prefer to attend? ...... (Why?)
Candidate A:	*[Approximately 30 seconds.]*
Interlocutor:	Thank you.

Parts 3 and 4   8 minutes (11 minutes for groups of three)

Part 3

The influence of friends

Interlocutor: Now, I'd like you to talk about something together for about two minutes *(3 minutes for groups of three)*.

Many people are too easily influenced by their friends. Here are some things to think about and a question for you to discuss. First you have some time to look at the task.

Indicate the text on page C12 to the candidates. Allow 15 seconds.

Now, talk to each other about whether you think people are too easily influenced by their friends.

Candidates: *[2 minutes (3 minutes for groups of three).]*

Interlocutor: Thank you. Now you have about a minute to decide what the best reason is for <u>not</u> being too easily influenced by your friends.

Candidates: *[1 minute (for pairs and groups of three).]*

Interlocutor: Thank you.

Part 4

Interlocutor: *Use the following questions, in order, as appropriate:*

- Some people say that we always want to have the same things as our friends. What do you think?

> *Select any of the following prompts, as appropriate:*
>
> - What do you think?
> - Do you agree?
> - And you?

- Do you think we can be friends with people who have very different ideas and opinions from us?

- Do you think it's better to have only one or two close friends or have a big group of friends? ...... (Why?)

- How important do you think it is for parents to like their children's friends?

- Some people think that the media influence us much more than our friends do. Do you agree? ...... (Why? / Why not?)

- Are we too easily influenced by people we have never met, such as sports stars or other famous people? ...... (Why do you say that?)

Thank you. That is the end of the test.

Marks and results

Reading and Use of English

Candidates record their answers on a separate answer sheet. One mark is given for each correct answer in Parts 1, 2, 3 and 7. For Part 4, candidates are awarded a mark of 2, 1 or 0 for each question according to the accuracy of their response. Correct spelling is required in Parts 2, 3 and 4. Two marks are given for each correct answer in Parts 5 and 6.

Candidates will receive separate scores for Reading and for Use of English. The total marks candidates achieve for each section are converted into a score on the Cambridge English Scale. These are equally weighted when calculating the overall score on the scale (an average of the individual scores for the four skills and Use of English).

Writing

Examiners look at four aspects of your writing: Content, Communicative Achievement, Organisation and Language.

- Content focuses on how well you have fulfilled the task, in other words if you have done what you were asked to do.
- Communicative Achievement focuses on how appropriate the writing is for the letter or story and whether you have used the appropriate register.
- Organisation focuses on the way you put the piece of writing together, in other words if it is logical and ordered, and the punctuation is correct.
- Language focuses on your vocabulary and grammar. This includes the range of language as well as how accurate it is.

For each of the subscales, the examiner gives a maximum of 5 marks. Examiners use the following assessment scale:

B2	Content	Communicative Achievement	Organisation	Language
5	All content is relevant to the task. Target reader is fully informed.	Uses the conventions of the communicative task effectively to hold the target reader's attention and communicate straightforward and complex ideas, as appropriate.	Text is well organised and coherent, using a variety of cohesive devices and organisational patterns to generally good effect.	Uses a range of vocabulary, including less common lexis, appropriately. Uses a range of simple and complex grammatical forms with control and flexibility. Occasional errors may be present but do not impede communication.
4	*Performance shares features of Bands 3 and 5.*			

3	Minor irrelevances and/or omissions may be present. Target reader is on the whole informed.	Uses the conventions of the communicative task to hold the target reader's attention and communicate straightforward ideas.	Text is generally well organised and coherent, using a variety of linking words and cohesive devices.	Uses a range of everyday vocabulary appropriately, with occasional inappropriate use of less common lexis. Uses a range of simple and some complex grammatical forms with a good degree of control. Errors do not impede communication.
2	*Performance shares features of Bands 1 and 3.*			
1	Irrelevances and misinterpretation of task may be present. Target reader is minimally informed.	Uses the conventions of the communicative task in generally appropriate ways to communicate straightforward ideas.	Text is connected and coherent, using basic linking words and a limited number of cohesive devices.	Uses everyday vocabulary generally appropriately, while occasionally overusing certain lexis. Uses simple grammatical forms with a good degree of control. While errors are noticeable, meaning can still be determined.
0	Content is totally irrelevant. Target reader is not informed.	*Performance below Band 1.*		

Length of responses

Make sure you write the correct number of words. Responses which are too short may not have an adequate range of language and may not provide all the information that is required. Responses which are too long may contain irrelevant content and have a negative effect on the reader.

Varieties of English

You are expected to use a particular variety of English with some degree of consistency in areas such as spelling, and not for example switch from using a British spelling of a word to an American spelling of the same word.

Writing sample answers and examiner's comments.

The following pieces of writing have been selected from students' answers. The samples relate to tasks in Tests 5–8. Explanatory notes have been added to show how the bands have been arrived at.

Sample A (Test 5, Question 1 – Essay)

> Nowadays empty playgrounds and pitches are commonly seen, whereas electronic shops are crowded and filled with groups of parents, who want to buy their children an entertainment. A modern way to entertain young people starts to get a brand new meaning, which is being shortened up to electronic gadgets. Do we participate in the new era of entertainment?
>
> Some people started to argue that these days relationships, who have children, spend much time to each carriers, regardless taking care of their children. From the very beginning of young life, the youths receive mobile phones, computers, playstations etc. from parents. They want to take off additional pressure and weight and choose the easiest way. On the other hand, parents are obligated to work hard in terms of financial situation and it is hard to make ends meet.
>
> What is more, modern entertainment creates a significant risk for impaired social relations. The more time you spend in front of a screen, the less sociable you become and they frequently fall into mental disorders.
>
> To sum up, I think that young people's entertainment is a real social danger. We have to sacrifice an enough amount of time to our children, unless it is not too late.

Scales	Mark	Commentary
Content	4	All content is relevant to the task. We learn about the causes and consequences of too much screen time, with detailed examples and explanations. The second content point, about books and reading, is not discussed and so the target reader is not fully informed.
Communicative Achievement	4	The conventions of essay writing are used effectively to communicate straightforward ideas. There is some attempt at expressing more complex ideas, although the language used is not always completely effective. The tone and register are appropriate and hold the target reader's attention.
Organisation	3	The text is generally well organised and coherent, making effective use of paragraphing for each new point. A variety of linking words and cohesive devices is used with reasonable success to connect ideas.
Language	3	A range of everyday vocabulary and some less common lexis (*brand new; gadgets; make ends meet; impaired social relations; mental disorders; sacrifice*) is used appropriately. There is a range of simple and some more complex grammatical forms used with a good degree of control. There are some errors with less common lexis (*shortened up to; relationships … who have children*) and grammatical structures (verb forms; *sacrifice an enough amount of time*), but these do not impede communication.

Sample B (Test 5, Question 3 – Report)

The aim of this report is to provide an overview of some problems in the Pascani's centre and to suggest what improvements should be made.

The already existing problems include the fact that there is no big shopping mall, just some little shops with aliments or clothes. The parking zone is also quite small and, as it is located in front of the Central Hotel, there is no space for all the cars. Not to mention the low level of cleanness around the zone where you can't even go for a walk.

It seems like the town centre has a lot of problems regarding its place. My recommendations are the following:

• building a new shopping centre which includes a variety of products and activities.

• enlarging the parking zone, so there will be more space for cars and for leisure activities of the young men too.

• cleaning up the zone and introducing recycle bins for the garbage

In the light of my suggestions, I strongly believe that these are the best methods of raising the pedestrians view of city.

Scales	Mark	Commentary
Content	5	All content is relevant and the target reader would be fully informed. The report describes several problems and suggests a range of solutions, giving reasons for why these would help improve the situation.
Communicative Achievement	4	The report has been written using the conventions of the genre, for example a clear introduction and conclusion and an objective and formal tone. Straightforward facts are supported by examples and explanations and bullet points are used to draw the reader's attention to key recommendations.
Organisation	4	The report is well organised and coherent, with effective use of paragraphing and punctuation to separate the key points. It makes use of a variety of cohesive devices to connect ideas within and across sentences and paragraphs.
Language	4	There is a range of task-specific vocabulary used appropriately (*an overview of some problems; My recommendations are the following; enlarging the parking zone; In the light of my suggestions*). There is a range of simple and more complex grammatical forms used with control. There are minimal errors and these do not impede.

Sample C (Test 6, Question 3 – Review)

My favourite TV series has to be Sherlock. It's an exciting and entertaining series based on short stories written by Arthur Connan Doyle.

The series displays how it would have been, had Sherlock Holmes lived in our modern era. Sherlock, the main character, is a consulting detective who offers help to desperate people who need to quickly find or recover something or someone. He often helps the advises the police forces of London to aid them when they're stuck with a case. His role in this British series is played by Benedict Cumberbetch. He always travels with his faithful companion, Dr. Henry Watson, who is played by Martin Freeman.

I love this series mainly because it's fun, while still remaining thrilling and mysterious. It has many references to the original novels and stories and manages to touch modern day problems as well. The only downside is that there are currently only 9 episodes within 3 series each being roughly about an hour and a half long.

I'd recommend Sherlock to anyone who's at least a little interested in the original books or who just likes detective stories with a tint of contemporary British humour.

Scales	Mark	Commentary
Content	5	All content is relevant to the task and the target reader would be fully informed. We learn about the series, what the writer likes about it and who they would recommend it to.
Communicative Achievement	4	The conventions of review writing are used effectively to communicate straightforward and some more complex ideas, for example the well-controlled summary of what the series is about in the second paragraph. The persuasive tone holds the reader's attention throughout.
Organisation	4	The text is well organised and coherent and makes use of a variety of suitable cohesive devices to introduce and connect the main points within and across sentences.
Language	5	There is a range of suitable, natural vocabulary, including less common lexis (*a consulting detective; stuck with a case; faithful companion; downside*) used appropriately. There is a range of simple and complex grammatical forms used with control. There are only occasional slips.

Sample D (Test 6, Question 4 – Letter)

> *Petrozavodsk*
> *Russia*
>
> *Dear Isobel,*
>
> *I have found you advertisment and would like to recommend myself as a guide to show Petrozavodsk.*
>
> *I know the town very well, because I often go for a walk with my friends, drive across town with my father and attend meetings in different parts of Petrozavodsk. I can easily explain you where is an object which you are interested in. You should only ask me what do you need: some street, monument, shop, cinema, club, cafe, park, hospital, museum and so on.*
>
> *Where are a lot of places where the students can stay. For example, they will be able to stay at one of hotels. But in my opinion such kind of accomodation can be quite expensive, because the students are coming for a week. So, I think it is possible to stay in the rooms for students of local university.*
>
> *I have been studying English for more than 10 years at school and attended extra classes, so my level of knowing the language is quite hard. You can hardly imagine how much hospitable and friendly people are living in our town, so I hope that your tour would be very useful and exciting.*

Scales	Mark	Commentary
Content	4	The target reader would be informed, but not fully. We learn a lot about why the writer would be suitable for the job and a little about places to visit in the town, but this point is underdeveloped and there is some irrelevance about accommodation in the third paragraph.
Communicative Achievement	4	The conventions of formal letter writing have been used effectively, despite the issues with opening and closing greetings, to hold the target reader's attention throughout. Straightforward ideas are expressed clearly and in a consistently formal and polite tone.
Organisation	3	The text is generally well organised and coherent with clear paragraphing, a variety of cohesive devices and a limited range of linking words.
Language	4	There is a range of vocabulary used appropriately, with only occasional slips with spelling and word choice (*advertisment; accomodation; my level ... is quite hard*). There is a range of simple and some more complex grammatical forms used with control. There are a few errors, but these do not impede communication.

Sample E (Test 7, Question 3 – Letter of application)

Dear Mr. Nick Jones,

I had been searching for a job when i discovered the advertisement in the local newpaper, in which you were offering a post at your holiday club.

I am an eighteen year-old student at King's College and I have a part-time job at the local library, as an assistant. In the last three years, I have been attending English courses and I have achieved a high score at an exam involving the language.

Since I started highschool, I have always enjoyed helping children in need. I was usually participating in children's parties as a helper, but I was also caring for the one's in the street by giving them food and by giving advice whenever they needed it.

I love children and I do my best to make them happy. I am comunicative, hard- working and patient.

In the end, I think I will manage with the challenges this job may offer. I inclose my curriculum vitae and a photography. I am looking forward to your reply!

yours sincerely,

Stefan Pasoi

Scales	Mark	Commentary
Content	5	All content is relevant to the task and the target reader would be fully informed. The reader learns in detail about the writer's experience of working with children and their knowledge of English.
Communicative Achievement	4	The conventions of formal letters of application are used generally effectively to communicate straightforward ideas. The tone is consistently formal and ideas are expressed clearly and persuasively to hold the target reader's attention throughout. Greater control and range of key language of letters of application, for example closing statements and greetings, would improve the overall effect on the reader.
Organisation	4	The text is well organised and coherent, making effective use of a variety of cohesive devices to introduce and connect ideas. There are good examples of internal cohesion, particularly in the third paragraph. Paragraphing is used effectively to present each key point.
Language	4	There is a range of topic-specific vocabulary which is generally used well (*an exam involving the language; helping children in need; as a helper*) and a range of simple and some more complex grammatical forms is used with a good degree of control. There are some errors, for example the inappropriate use of the exclamation mark, with spelling and the choice of past tense, but these do not impede communication.

Sample F (Test 7, Question 4 – Article)

I think you would agree that ambition has a big influance on our lifes. But what really mean to be ambitious? How important is ambition in a daily life?

From my point of view it is very hard to talk about ambition. I have many ambitions. I want to be well-educated and sporty. I believe that these aims are good for me because I have to try to achieve them all the time. They make that I am not a lazy person. Good ambitions do not let us stop working and learning.

But what happen when we are too ambitious? I know many people who think that their ambitions, ideas and aims are the most important think in their life. It is a beautiful idea but we have to know where is the border. We cannot forget about other people when we are intending to achieve our ambition we must remember to stay a human for example, I spend a lot of time learning but I often prefer to go for a trip with my parents even if I will get a bad mark.

To sum up, ambition is very important in my life but I know there are many things which I value more like my family. I want to achieve my ambitions but it would not be a big loss for me do not do it.

Scales	Mark	Commentary
Content	3	The target reader is on the whole informed despite minor irrelevance and omissions. We learn about what ambition means to the writer and, briefly, about the writer's own ambitions. Details about how the writer intends to achieve their ambitions have been omitted and there is some irrelevance in the paragraph on problems with being too ambitious.
Communicative Achievement	4	The conventions of writing an article are used effectively to communicate ideas using an engaging tone. The use of rhetorical questions and the balance between general statements and personal opinions hold the reader's attention throughout.
Organisation	3	The text is generally well organised and coherent with a clear introduction and logical development of the topic, making use of paragraphs, a variety of linking words and some cohesive devices, such as referencing and substitution. Some attempt is made at connecting ideas in longer sentences, for example the final sentence of the third paragraph.
Language	3	A range of everyday vocabulary suitable for the task is used appropriately (*well-educated; sporty; intending to achieve; it would not be a big loss*). There is a range of simple and some more complex grammatical forms used with a good degree of control. Some errors with lexis and sentence structure are present, but they do not impede communication.

Sample G (Test 8, Question 1 – Essay)

> A very common topic that is being discussed nowadays is wether schools should teach subjects that some may consider useless later in life. A clear example is history, since it is quite difficult to learn and does not help us in day-to-day activities.
>
> However, many people do not realize the importance of it or that it affects our lives today. For example, our political system would not be this way if it weren't for the Ancient Greeks, numerous politicians and wars who helped shape democracy and our constitution. Yet it is still thought that it's useless.
>
> In addition, it is very important that we never forget about our past since we must know where we were standing years ago. Moreover, there are some things, such as World War II, that we have to remember to prevent them from happening again. We should also know where we we were standing a century ago: our origins, our identity. The more you learn about your ethnicity, the better.
>
> All in all, I think that it is extremely important to learn about one's own country's history. Anyone who gets the chance to do this should not waste it, since they are very fortunate to have this opportunity.

Scales	Mark	Commentary
Content	5	All content is relevant to the task and the target reader is fully informed. The first two points have been discussed together in detail and a third point, about origins and identity, has been included.
Communicative Achievement	5	The conventions of essay writing have been used effectively to discuss the issues in an informed manner. Straightforward and some more complex ideas, for example the point about the Ancient Greeks and the closing statement, are communicated using an engaging tone which is suitable for a wide audience and which holds the reader's attention throughout.
Organisation	5	The text is well organised and coherent and makes effective use of a variety of cohesive devices to skilfully connect ideas both within and across sentences and paragraphs. Some organisational patterns are used to good effect, for example the parallel short statements ending the third and fourth paragraphs.
Language	5	There is a range of vocabulary, including less common lexis (*numerous politicians; shape democracy and our constitution; our origins, our identity; your ethnicity*) used appropriately. There is a range of simple and complex grammatical forms used with control and flexibility. Errors, mainly related to less common lexis, are minimal.

Sample H (Test 8, Question 3 – Email)

Dear Susan,

I think you know from the start that this subject may be inappropriate to discuss with me, but since we are best friends, I accept.

If I were you, I would spend it all on an amazing holiday with my friends where you can do fun things and maybe meat someone special..

I am not sure what you are supposed to do with the money, but I can help you find the best solution. You must think simultaniously at both advantages and disadvantages. If you give your money to your parents, you would loose the benefits from it, but you could also help them.

I suggest you put it in your bank account and wait until celebrities can show up at your door, so that you can photograph them and be well-known.

There are a lot of money, so think carefully which is the best solution. You can also contact me or meat face-to-face if you need.

Therefore, you can benefit from it if you are wise and rational

Yours,

Andrea

Scales	Mark	Commentary
Content	5	All content is relevant to the task and the target reader is fully informed. All options are considered in detail and a clear viewpoint is presented.
Communicative Achievement	3	The conventions of writing an informal email are used to communicate straightforward advice. A friendly, natural tone is used throughout to hold the target reader's attention.
Organisation	3	The text is generally well organised and coherent. Ideas are introduced and connected mainly at sentence level using a variety of linking words and some cohesive devices.
Language	3	Everyday vocabulary is used appropriately, with some attempt at less common lexis (*may be inappropriate; simultaniously; show up at your door; wise and rational*). There is a range of simple grammatical forms used appropriately and with a good degree of control. Errors, mainly with spelling, do not impede communication.

Listening

One mark is given for each correct answer. The total mark is converted into a score on the Cambridge English Scale for the paper. In **Part 2**, minor spelling errors are allowed, provided that the candidate's intention is clear.

For security reasons, several versions of the Listening paper are used at each administration of the examination. Before grading, the performance of the candidates in each of the versions is compared and marks adjusted to compensate for any imbalance in levels of difficulty.

Speaking

Throughout the test candidates are assessed on their own individual performance and not in relation to the other candidate. They are assessed on their language skills, not on their personality, intelligence or knowledge of the world. Candidates must, however, be prepared to develop the conversation and respond to the tasks in an appropriate way.

Candidates are awarded marks by two examiners: the assessor and the interlocutor. The assessor awards marks by applying performance descriptors from the Analytical Assessment scales for the following criteria:

Grammar and Vocabulary
This refers to the accurate use of grammatical forms and appropriate use of vocabulary. It also includes the range of language.

Discourse Management
This refers to the extent, relevance and coherence of each candidate's contributions. Candidates should be able to construct clear stretches of speech which are easy to follow. The length of their contributions should be appropriate to the task, and what they say should be related to the topic and the conversation in general.

Pronunciation
This refers to the intelligibility of contributions at word and sentence levels. Candidates should be able to produce utterances that can easily be understood, and which show control of intonation, stress and individual sounds.

Interactive Communication
This refers to the ability to use language to achieve meaningful communication. Candidates should be able to initiate and respond appropriately according to the task and conversation, and also to use interactive strategies to maintain and develop the communication whilst negotiating towards an outcome.

B2	Grammar and Vocabulary	Discourse Management	Pronunciation	Interactive Communication
5	• Shows a good degree of control of a range of simple and some complex grammatical forms. • Uses a range of appropriate vocabulary to give and exchange views on a wide range of familiar topics.	• Produces extended stretches of language with very little hesitation. • Contributions are relevant and there is a clear organisation of ideas. • Uses a range of cohesive devices and discourse markers.	• Is intelligible. • Intonation is appropriate. • Sentence and word stress is accurately placed. • Individual sounds are articulated clearly.	• Initiates and responds appropriately, linking contributions to those of other speakers. • Maintains and develops the interaction and negotiates towards an outcome.
4	*Performance shares features of Bands 3 and 5.*			
3	• Shows a good degree of control of simple grammatical forms, and attempts some complex grammatical forms. • Uses a range of appropriate vocabulary to give and exchange views on a range of familiar topics.	• Produces extended stretches of language despite some hesitation. • Contributions are relevant and there is very little repetition. • Uses a range of cohesive devices.	• Is intelligible. • Intonation is generally appropriate. • Sentence and word stress is generally accurately placed. • Individual sounds are generally articulated clearly.	• Initiates and responds appropriately. • Maintains and develops the interaction and negotiates towards an outcome with very little support.
2	*Performance shares features of Bands 1 and 3.*			
1	• Shows a good degree of control of simple grammatical forms. • Uses a range of appropriate vocabulary when talking about everyday situations.	• Produces responses which are extended beyond short phrases, despite hesitation. • Contributions are mostly relevant, despite some repetition. • Uses basic cohesive devices.	• Is mostly intelligible, and has some control of phonological features at both utterance and word levels.	• Initiates and responds appropriately. • Keeps the interaction going with very little prompting and support.
0	*Performance below Band 1.*			

The interlocutor awards a mark for overall performance using a Global Achievement scale.

B2	Global Achievement
5	• Handles communication on a range of familiar topics, with very little hesitation. • Uses accurate and appropriate linguistic resources to express ideas and produce extended discourse that is generally coherent.
4	*Performance shares features of Bands 3 and 5.*
3	• Handles communication on familiar topics, despite some hesitation. • Organises extended discourse but occasionally produces utterances that lack coherence, and some inaccuracies and inappropriate usage occur.
2	*Performance shares features of Bands 1 and 3.*
1	• Handles communication in everyday situations, despite hesitation. • Constructs longer utterances but is not able to use complex language except in well-rehearsed utterances.
0	*Performance below Band 1.*

Assessment for *Cambridge English: First* is based on performance across all parts of the test, and is achieved by applying the relevant descriptors in the assessment scales.

Test 5 Key

Reading and Use of English (1 hour 15 minutes)

Part 1

1 D   2 A   3 C   4 B   5 D   6 A   7 B   8 B

Part 2

9 after   10 though   11 where   12 carry/keep   13 do   14 since
15 who   16 order

Part 3

17 nearby   18 knowledge   19 width   20 investigation(s)   21 originally
22 discovery   23 evidence   24 unsure

Part 4

25 up my MIND | about OR my MIND up | about
26 paid (any / the slightest / the least / much) ATTENTION | to
27 WOULD have | rung/called/(tele)phoned
28 is n't/not cancelled | DUE to
29 in the MOOD | for
30 he'd / he had | RUN into

Part 5

31 C   32 D   33 B   34 C   35 A   36 D

Part 6

37 E   38 A   39 G   40 B   41 D   42 F

Part 7

43 D   44 A   45 D   46 A   47 C   48 A   49 C   50 D   51 A
52 B

Writing (1 hour 20 minutes)

Candidate responses are marked using the assessment scale on pages 107–108.

Listening (approximately 40 minutes)

Part 1

1 A   2 C   3 C   4 B   5 C   6 A   7 B   8 A

Part 2

9 (local) charity   10 industry   11 lawyer   12 chocolate   13 passport
14 concert   15 (gold) medal (each)   16 problem-solving / solving problems
17 social worker   18 information pack

Part 3

19 D   20 H   21 F   22 G   23 C

Part 4

24 A   25 C   26 C   27 B   28 A   29 B   30 C

Transcript

This is the Cambridge English: First Listening Test. Test Five.

I am going to give you the instructions for this test. I shall introduce each part of the test and give you time to look at the questions. At the start of each piece you will hear this sound:

tone

You will hear each piece twice.

Remember, while you are listening, write your answers on the question paper. You will have five minutes at the end of the test to copy your answers onto the separate answer sheet.

There will now be a pause. Please ask any questions now, because you must not speak during the test.

[pause]

Now open your question paper and look at Part One.

[pause]

PART 1   *You will hear people talking in eight different situations. For questions 1 to 8, choose the best answer (A, B or C).*

Question 1   *You hear part of an interview with a crime writer.*

[pause]

tone

Interviewer: You came from quite a tough town, didn't you?

Man: Yes, I did. The experiences I had living there, the people I know, the lessons I had to learn growing up have stood me in good stead for the kind of life I've chosen. I'm streetwise as a result of all that and I feel equipped to write the crime novels that I'm known for. I definitely haven't lived a sheltered life. I still have to go back there a lot to see family. Luckily, as a writer, my face isn't that well known. It's not as if I'm a celebrity with my name on the cover of every magazine.

[pause]

tone

[The recording is repeated.]

[pause]

Question 2   *You hear a careers advisor talking to a woman who has applied for two jobs.*

[pause]

tone

Woman: I've been for two job interviews and I've been offered the first job. I'd prefer the second one but I haven't heard from the company yet. What should I do?

Advisor: It's difficult to make the right decision if you don't have all the information to hand. I'd explain to the first employer that you're very pleased to have been offered the job but some other organisations haven't been in touch with you yet. Ask them if it's possible to have a bit more time before you decide. Hopefully, they'll be understanding. Just remember that there could be legal consequences if you accept the first job in writing and then turn it down!

[pause]

tone

[The recording is repeated.]

[pause]

Question 3   *You hear a girl talking about a psychology text book.*

[pause]

tone

Well I was quite excited when I finally found this psychology book, because I need it for my assignment. It was hardly cheap, and I know I could get a lot of the information in it for free online, but I still think it was worth getting my own copy of it. It has such clear explanations – I probably won't find anything else as useful. Some books like this can turn out to be pretty boring, I know, but I just don't believe this one will. And it's no more expensive than any of the other coursebooks I have to buy.

[pause]

tone

[The recording is repeated.]

[pause]

Question 4   *You hear the mother of a famous skier talking about a competition.*

[pause]

tone

Well, I don't know who was more surprised, Kelly or me, that she'd won. She didn't start skiing until she was fourteen so she was quite a late starter really. She went to work in a restaurant in Austria in the year before she went to university and went skiing every day after work. I tried to get in touch with her one day at the restaurant and couldn't – she'd left apparently. Then a couple of days later, she phoned me and said, "Guess what? I've got a new job in a different restaurant, but more importantly, I've just won the junior skiing championship!". I couldn't believe it!

[pause]

tone

[The recording is repeated.]

[pause]

Question 5   *You hear a film director talking about the actors she works with.*

[pause]

tone

I have to say, having also worked on some very big-budget films, there are all sorts of advantages to working on a small project like this one. Everyone shares a common goal. Actors always have three reasons to act. The first is to make money for their family, the second is to do good work and the third is to get their name in lights. The main actors, Chris and Fiona, are already big names in showbusiness. I don't think they're short of money either. No, they're doing this because they're totally committed to the project.

[pause]

tone

[The recording is repeated.]

[pause]

Question 6   *You hear a man talking about his first job interview.*

[pause]

tone

I'd read everything I could about the company and referred to a lot of it in my interview. I wanted the interviewer to know how much research I'd done and how much I wanted the job and I'd thought about what an interviewer would want to know about me based on what I could offer. Deep down I knew I'd be a great match. In the interview there was a long silence after one question I was asked but I knew it was important not to say the first thing that came into my head. I did say a few embarrassing things but I just moved on.

[pause]

tone

[The recording is repeated.]

[pause]

Question 7 *You hear two friends talking about a popular television programme.*

[pause]

tone

Man: Did you watch that programme last night on Channel Two?

Woman: Yeah. It's hard to believe Helen Jenkins is seventy-five years old, isn't it? Most people give up work well before then and she still seems to be on TV all the time!

Man: I know! I think it's because she's such a good communicator and she's come into her own, hasn't she, with the move away from complicated cuisine towards the simple, budget-friendly family stuff. It's very much in keeping with the times, isn't it?

Woman: Yes, but I still haven't learnt to do it myself.

[pause]

tone

[The recording is repeated.]

[pause]

Question 8 *You hear two people talking about a place they have visited.*

[pause]

tone

Woman: I loved the architecture, didn't you?

Man: Yeah, it was so unusual – I mean when you think of what's being put up in cities nowadays – you know, all the shopping centres and places, then you wonder whether anyone actually bothers to design buildings like that anymore.

Woman: That's right, and it's just so quiet and peaceful in there – you could really take time to look at all the objects on display. I loved those rare fifteenth-century books! So different from anything you could ever buy.

Man: Yeah, me too. I'm going to read up on those now, in fact. There'll be something about them on the internet, or maybe a book I can borrow.

[pause]

tone

[The recording is repeated.]

[pause]

That is the end of Part One.

Now turn to Part Two.

[pause]

PART 2

You will hear a girl called Laura Beamer talking about being a volunteer at a summer school for seven to fourteen year olds, which is called the Children's University. For questions 9 to 18, complete the sentences with a word or short phrase.

You now have forty-five seconds to look at Part Two.

[pause]

tone

I'm here today to talk about a wonderful project I've been involved in this summer called the Children's University. It's run every day for local children aged from seven to fourteen by a team of parents, teachers, students and local employers. It was originally set up by a local charity and has been running for the last five years.

The aim of the Children's University is to inspire children and foster a love of learning. It sounds rather grand I know, but it was amazing to watch the children working so enthusiastically on all the various projects. This year the topic and overall theme was industry, building on previous years' themes such as culture and science.

Each volunteer on the scheme was partnered with another with a different background. I was paired up with Mark, who was fantastic at motivating the children. He was a natural teacher and the children really loved him. Not exactly what you'd expect from a lawyer! I'm a student at university doing biology so we couldn't have been more different!

The workshop material was written by the volunteers. I was in a group of six who taught a series of workshops on manufacturing in our city called Making Chocolate. The workshop included taking the children to visit the local factory and we even had a tasting session! Other groups did things like making their own furniture and baking bread.

Each child had their own booklet which was stamped when they'd successfully finished a project. This was known by everybody as their 'passport'. The children were very competitive and were always comparing to see who'd collected the most stamps. It really seemed to be much more effective in encouraging the children to do more workshops than last year when group leaders simply signed their notebook each time they did a workshop.

At the end of the Children's University we held a graduation ceremony in the city's real university. This was held in the Concert Hall and was very exciting for the children. They all wore graduation caps and gowns. And afterwards, everyone went to the dining hall for the official photos and refreshments. It was just like a proper graduation ceremony and the children and their parents loved it.

Every child that attended the Children's University was awarded a certificate. In addition, the children who had attended the most workshops received a gold medal each. Some had been to as many as forty workshops over the summer!

The main benefit for me of volunteering for the Children's University was learning from the other volunteers because many of them were older than me and more experienced. For example, I had ample opportunity to practise problem-solving and became much better at it. It's a useful skill that I can use in the workplace when I graduate.

Another benefit is that it gave me the opportunity to work with children. I'd been undecided about whether to become a teacher or a social worker. While I loved helping the children learn, the experience has confirmed that what I most want to do is help children and their families in our community who are having difficulties.

I think that having worked on the Children's University should definitely help me after I graduate and want to start my career because I can show that I've got experience of working closely with children. I'm definitely going to do it again next summer.

If you think this kind of work is for you, and would like to register for next summer, come and ask me for an information pack after this talk. When you're sure it's what you want to do, you can download an application form from the Children's University website.

[pause]

Now you will hear Part Two again.

[Teacher, repeat the track now.]

[pause]

That is the end of Part Two.

Now turn to Part Three.

[pause]

PART 3

You will hear five different people talking about why they have applied to go on a space journey to the planet Mars. For questions 19 to 23, choose from the list (A to H) each speaker's reason for applying to go on the trip to Mars. Use the letters only once. There are three extra letters which you do not need to use.

You now have thirty seconds to look at Part Three.

[pause]

tone

Speaker 1

When they went to the moon, they brought back samples of moon rock that turned out to be really important in various fields of physics and chemistry. That's the main thing for me really – what we can gain from going to Mars. I don't know exactly what kind of person they're looking for but I'd be gutted if I'm not it! I don't think they want celebrities or anyone like that. They want people who are really committed to space travel, like me. I studied astronomy at university and I've been fascinated by it ever since.

[pause]

Speaker 2

To me, the chance to go somewhere no one else has ever been, a planet completely different from the one that every person who has ever lived has known, clinched it for me. Of course, leaving my family will be hard but there will be regular video and computer links for personal use in space, so it'll be OK. There are lots of theories about how life may once have existed on Mars – but I don't know too much about that. I do think that I'll see the Earth and all the people on it differently once I've seen it from space. It'll be so inspiring.

[pause]

Speaker 3

I think it takes a particular type of person to even consider a trip to Mars. And I don't mean you <u>have</u> to have a brilliant scientific mind, or anything like that. You have to be someone who wants to push themselves to the limit. That's exactly the sort of person I am, and that's why this adventure appeals to me. I've also got some very useful practical skills, because I'm a mechanical engineer. So I think I'd be able to contribute a lot to the team.

[pause]

Speaker 4

I think it'll have such a huge impact on the whole world. It's an amazing opportunity to make scientific discoveries. For me though, it's about providing young people with positive role models and this project will really catch their imagination. It shouldn't be about wanting your name in lights or doing something no one else has done before. Yes, it'll be scary but I trust the people who have the knowledge to keep us safe. The most difficult thing for me will be going without fresh fruit and vegetables.

[pause]

Speaker 5

I've always dreamt of travelling into space but of course I know it won't be easy. What'll get me through is the knowledge that this will have a huge impact on the entire planet. I think I'll see things differently too as a result of this trip. But the main thing is an adventure like this only ever comes up once in a lifetime and I'd be insane to pass it up! I haven't actually been to many places where I've had to rely on my own skills to survive but I'm sure that they'll teach us everything we'll need to know.

[pause]

Now you will hear Part Three again.

tone

[The recording is repeated.]

[pause]

That is the end of Part Three.

Now turn to Part Four.

[pause]

PART 4   *You will hear an interview with a man called Mark Phillips, who is talking about his work as a potter. For questions 24 to 30, choose the best answer (A, B or C).*

You now have one minute to look at Part Four.

[pause]

tone

Interviewer: My guest today is the potter Mark Phillips whose first exhibition opens in the Carlisle Gallery on Friday. Welcome. I know you've only been a potter for four years so you must be pleased to have this exhibition.

Mark: I'm thrilled. And you're right, this is something fairly new for me. When I was younger I never wanted to be a potter. You see, my mother was a very successful one and I used to watch her in her studio. I could admire the way she created beautiful things from lumps of clay but I just remember thinking how on earth could I ever hope to reach that standard? I was more into playing music with my friends – we had grand ideas about forming a band. But you know, that was something we never got around to doing!

Interviewer: So what made you change your mind and take up pottery?

Mark: I was forty years old with my own computer company that I'd set up when I left school, and I was feeling a bit – you know – stuck. And I kind of reasoned with myself that the artistic side of me had been buried for quite long enough. My mother suggested pottery evening classes and came up with a whole load of ways they'd benefit me. I guess I had my doubts about whether doing it once a week in the evening would be satisfying.

Interviewer: So, at the age of forty, you went to college and became a student again.

Mark: I did. It was strange at first. I had no deadlines to keep to. My brain was still working obviously, but it was my body that was now being exercised – and you need a lot of stamina to be a potter. That was a big plus for me after sitting at a computer for years. I think my fellow students, who were all in their twenties, were surprised to see this older man, full of enthusiasm and working hard. But I loved it.

Interviewer: And how would you describe your pots?

Mark: Well, most of them are made on the wheel, but just lately I've been hand-building. I make the pot using pieces of clay that I flatten by rolling them out – a bit like making pastry – then I press my knife into the clay to make a pattern: stars, triangles, whatever. Leaves would be ideal, but my mother might object, as that's her specialty! Like mom's, my pots are practical things. They shouldn't just be on a shelf somewhere being admired in a sitting room.

Interviewer: And how have your fellow potters reacted to your success?

Mark: You mean, are they jealous? I've seen no evidence of that. Potters are generally quite interested in what fellow potters are doing. Obviously a lot of them knew my mother's work and they've been nothing but helpful to me on a practical level such as letting me use their kiln to fire my pots in, something that I never imagined would happen. Very few potters earn much money – it's hard enough making the pots, but then you've got to get yourself known in order for people to want to buy them.

Interviewer: Does your mother take an interest in your work and give you advice?

Mark: Of course and she's usually right. She was worried when I gave up my computer company because I'd been making good money, so she insisted I invested some of it for my old age! Also, she's always told me to look at the pots made by potters in history, sometimes going back thousands of years. If there's one single thing that's really inspired me, I guess that'd be it. It keeps me focused on keeping things simple, not being too ambitious with the shapes I make.

Interviewer: And after this exhibition is over, what do you think you'll be doing?

Mark: Oh that's hard. I'm still new to this and I'm keen to learn more – really big pots are what I want to make but I have to get to grips with learning how to do that. Also the gallery tell me that some customers want pots in bright colours so that's something I'll pass on to my mother. That's more her thing because it's much more complicated than it sounds.

Interviewer: Thank you, Mark … [fade]

[pause]

Now you will hear Part Four again.

[Teacher, repeat the track now.]

[pause]

That is the end of Part Four.

There will now be a pause of five minutes for you to copy your answers onto the separate answer sheet. Be sure to follow the numbering of all the questions. I shall remind you when there is one minute left, so that you are sure to finish in time.

That is the end of the test. Please stop now. Your supervisor will now collect all the question papers and answer sheets.

Test 6 Key

Reading and Use of English (1 hour 15 minutes)

Part 1

1 A   2 C   3 D   4 B   5 C   6 B   7 D   8 B

Part 2

9 at/during/in   10 was/became   11 course   12 it   13 in   14 more   15 and
16 which/that

Part 3

17 enjoyable   18 fortunate   19 difference   20 excitement   21 height
22 unlike   23 choice   24 spectacular

Part 4

25 the only PERSON | that/who did
26 CONCERNS me | is
27 had/'d stayed/waited/remained | UNTIL the end
28 was an | INCREASE in
29 CATCH up | on/with (all) your/the
30 few meals | AS good as

Part 5

31 B   32 B   33 A   34 B   35 C   36 B

Part 6

37 D   38 A   39 G   40 C   41 F   42 E

Part 7

43 C   44 A   45 D   46 D   47 B   48 D   49 B   50 A   51 C   52 D

Writing (1 hour 20 minutes)

Candidate responses are marked using the assessment scale on pages 107–108.

Listening (approximately 40 minutes)

Part 1

1 A   2 C   3 B   4 C   5 A   6 A   7 B   8 B

Part 2

9 cousin   10 roof   11 sport(s)   12 singer   13 violins   14 magazine
15 museum   16 typing   17 canteen   18 radio station

Part 3

19 C   20 A   21 G   22 D   23 F

Part 4

24 C   25 B   26 B   27 A   28 A   29 C   30 B

Transcript

This is the Cambridge English: First Listening Test. Test Six.

I am going to give you the instructions for this test. I shall introduce each part of the test and give you time to look at the questions. At the start of each piece you will hear this sound:

tone

You will hear each piece twice.

Remember, while you are listening, write your answers on the question paper. You will have five minutes at the end of the test to copy your answers onto the separate answer sheet.

There will now be a pause. Please ask any questions now, because you must not speak during the test.

[pause]

Now open your question paper and look at Part One.

[pause]

PART 1   *You will hear people talking in eight different situations. For questions 1 to 8, choose the best answer (A, B or C).*

Question 1   *You hear a psychologist talking about green spaces in cities.*

[pause]

tone

I'd like to start my talk today about green spaces in cities by acknowledging the fact that more and more governments are coming to accept that they are a vital element of a healthy society. Whether you're an adult, a teenager, or a young child, parks play a crucial role in ensuring our wellbeing. Yet too few of us really understand that, and as a society, we tend not to make enough use of the ones we already have. So when it comes to planning decisions, there just isn't enough pressure on local authorities to incorporate them in the future development of our cities. The consequences are potentially very serious.

[pause]

tone

[The recording is repeated.]

[pause]

Question 2   *You hear part of an interview with a singer.*

[pause]

tone

I play a lot of tennis because staying in good physical shape is absolutely vital if you're a singer or a musician. When I'm playing tennis, I always think how much it has in common with singing. For example, playing tennis, you learn how to concentrate, develop self-control and of course how to pace your breath and maximise the use of your energy. Before I have a big concert in the evening I'll often have a quick game of tennis just to relax. It can't be too energetic though or I wouldn't be able to give a good performance!

[pause]

tone

[The recording is repeated.]

[pause]

Question 3   *You hear an actor talking about how she met her husband.*

[pause]

tone

Well, Jonny, my husband, happened to hear me being interviewed on the radio and thought I'd be good for the part of the heroine in a play he was about to appear in. So he persuaded the director to send me the script. I liked it, we met on stage at the rehearsals, fell in love, and the rest is history. I'd seen Jonny perform before and admired his work but I didn't accept the part just because he was in it. I did know he was a nice person though, because a friend of mine had sat next to him at a film premiere and had told me about him.

[pause]

tone

[The recording is repeated.]

[pause]

Question 4   *You hear two people talking about a bus service.*

[pause]

tone

Man: Do you ever use the bus between Boroughbridge and Malton?

Woman: No, is it any good?

Man: Could be worse, I suppose, but I can't say it's cheap. You can save a bit by buying a season ticket, but not actually that much.

Woman: Really?

Man: Well what it does have in its favour is that it's very rarely late. Although it's a shame it only runs every three quarters of an hour.

Woman: I'll stick to my motorbike, then!

Man: You can't read your book on that, though, can you?

Woman: No, true, but I like to get to places quickly!

[pause]

tone

[The recording is repeated.]

[pause]

Question 5   *You hear a retired ballerina comparing dancers today with dancers in the past.*

[pause]

tone

Nowadays, ballet is much more acrobatic than in the past. The audience wants to see internationally famous dancers doing lots of jumps and legs going remarkably high. It's a bit more like a circus now, and the depth of feeling that we tried to convey in the past isn't always there in modern ballet. You only find it in one or two dancers. I'd love to see less focus on technique. I usually come away from watching a ballet feeling impressed with what I've seen but it hasn't moved me.

[pause]

tone

[The recording is repeated.]

[pause]

Question 6   *You hear a chef talking about making a TV series.*

[pause]

tone

I was approached to do a TV cookery series, where I had to compete against another chef every week. Never having met him before, I was a bit apprehensive about working with him. But we got on like a house on fire. It's rare for me to spend ten hours a day with someone for five weeks and like them more by the end of it than I did at the beginning. Halfway through filming the producer had to ring me up and ask if we could be less friendly with one another on camera, because it was supposed to be a competition!

[pause]

tone

[The recording is repeated.]

[pause]

Question 7   *You hear two friends talking about an art course.*

[pause]

tone

Woman: So are you enjoying the art course?

Man: I am, I think. I mean, what we're actually learning about is interesting – what inspired the nineteenth-century French painters and that sort of thing.

Woman: I feel I've heard it all before – I'd hoped the teacher would tell us more about their actual techniques. But at least there aren't too many of us on the course.

Man: That certainly helps when it comes to group discussions and stuff. And the teacher's amazing, don't you think?

Woman: He certainly thinks he is – I'm not convinced! I just don't feel very motivated at the moment, to be honest.

[pause]

tone

[The recording is repeated.]

[pause]

Question 8   *You hear a swimmer talking about a competition she took part in.*

[pause]

tone

I had such a good time at the championships, better than I expected. The atmosphere was incredible with everyone cheering. I didn't expect so many people to turn up to the event, though I don't suppose they were there to see me. I hadn't been too happy with my performance in the previous competition, so to turn things round like that was very satisfying. The pressure started to get to me at one point, but I had a talk with myself and got things into perspective. I must work on my nerves before the next big event, but I can't wait to get back in the pool and start training for it.

[pause]

tone

[The recording is repeated.]

[pause]

That is the end of Part One.

Now turn to Part Two.

[pause]

PART 2   *You will hear a man called Sid Holmes talking about a journalism course he attended. For questions 9 to 18, complete the sentences with a word or short phrase.*

You now have forty-five seconds to look at Part Two.

[pause]

tone

Hi, my name's Sid Holmes, and I'm here to talk about my experiences studying journalism at Kramer's College.

I decided to do journalism because my aunt, who's a newspaper reporter herself, advised me to do it. And I heard all about how good the Kramer's course was from my cousin, who'd been a student on it.

On the first day of the course we did some reporting exercises which I just couldn't get my head around. How do you write in fifty words about someone getting stuck on a roof and having to be lifted off by helicopter? But that was what I had to try and do! Another group had to do the same thing – about someone being stuck in a tree and rescued by boat.

We also met someone called Lisa on the first day. She works on a local paper and gave us some very informative talks throughout the course on what life is really like as a journalist. She's an assistant editor – every newspaper section has one. She started off in the fashion section as a junior reporter, but is now in sports and enjoying that more. Her aim is to run the news section one day.

Our main tutor on the course, Jim Tyler, who did most of the teaching, was great – I was particularly impressed to find out that not only was he an experienced journalist but also an accomplished painter, who'd had his work in quite a few local exhibitions. And he'd actually written a book too – about the life of a singer who's well known internationally, but is actually originally from our area.

Jim asked us to come up with ideas for articles, and then we all discussed them as a group. Someone mentioned this guy who makes watches and sells them online – that reminded me I'd heard about a retired teacher who'd taken up making violins. He doesn't sell them but lends them to talented schoolchildren. Jim said he thought that was a great idea. He said he'd recently written about a craftsman too – a man who makes shoes.

So off I went to write my first article! I finished it in a day, and emailed it to a few people, you know – newspapers, websites and so on, as we'd been told to do. Amazingly, one magazine got back to me just a week later and said they'd put it in their next issue! So a month later, my work was in print!

Because you have to do lots of work experience on the course, we were each sent off to report on different council meetings in the town hall. Not exactly exciting, but good practice I suppose. Some of the others had to write about the town park or even the shopping centre. I went to one about a community group's plans to make the museum more attractive to visitors – it would be great for the town if their proposals were adopted, so I actually enjoyed that.

Although on the whole, the course was fantastic, there were inevitably a few things that were less so. I mean, compared to learning all about photography, the typing lessons were pretty dull! I know they will come in useful, though, so I suppose I shouldn't complain.

The other students on the course were cool – we got on very well, and after lessons we'd often meet up. If a few of us were around at lunchtime, we'd get together in the canteen – the food was pretty good, made with produce from the college garden. We'd discuss what we were working on and that was a great help when I was stuck for inspiration.

So now, I'm doing a bit of freelance stuff and looking for a job! It's tough, and I've already been turned down for three jobs on news websites. I've got another interview next week, though, as a junior reporter for a radio station. It'd be amazing if I got that!

So, have any of you got any questions? …

[pause]

Now you will hear Part Two again.

[Teacher, repeat the track now.]

[pause]

That is the end of Part Two.

Now turn to Part Three.

[pause]

PART 3

You will hear five short extracts in which people are talking about collecting things as a hobby. For questions 19 to 23, choose from the list (A to H) why each speaker collects the things. Use the letters only once. There are three extra letters which you do not need to use.

You now have thirty seconds to look at Part Three.

[pause]

tone

Speaker 1

I collect toys from all over the world, and have done for about five years now. I spend a lot of time on it, trawling the internet for rare ones and going to toy fairs at the weekend. Some of the toys I've found are very beautiful. I have a busy job, so it's hard to make time for it sometimes. But it's great because there are so many different collectors out there, from all walks of life, who are fascinating to talk to. It's the social side of it that appeals to me, really. And it's taught me so much about how parents in different countries bring up their children.

[pause]

Speaker 2

My passion is coins. I've met a few people who've been surprised when I told them that! It takes up most of my spare time, but I don't mind – I get such a sense of achievement when I've finally tracked down a really rare coin. It wouldn't be nearly so much fun if there was less effort involved. Sometimes I give one or two away – to friends, you know – if I have two or three of the same type, then it's a nice thing to do. Some of the coins in my collection are hundreds of years old.

[pause]

Speaker 3

My magazine collection's getting bigger all the time. I read every one of them from cover to cover, which is time consuming and unfortunately means I have less time to spend with my children. The magazines are all about things I'm keen on, of course, like sports and cars. I'm very interested in how attitudes to sports have changed over time, and like to feel that link between life, say, fifty years ago, and the present day. It's quite a valuable collection now, so I keep it in a locked room to be on the safe side. I certainly have no plans to give my collection away, and I don't want to lose it!

[pause]

Speaker 4

Postcards are amazing things to collect, and I have over a thousand now.
I know people tend to communicate online, but a surprising number of
people still send them! It's not just about the pictures on the front, but what's
written on the back, too. Lots just have the usual stuff, like 'Weather good,
food great', but I look out for ones with a story, or glimpses of a story. My
collection is relatively modern, but I imagine historians in the future could
learn a lot from them. That's my aim really, to make them available to the
public one day – I'll donate them to my local museum.

[pause]

Speaker 5

I'm crazy about hats: smart men's hats, caps, anything like that. They aren't
beautiful, like some women's hats, but wherever I go in the world, and I've
travelled quite a lot, I bring another one home with me. It's quite a large
collection now, and I've been told it's worth quite a lot. That's mainly why I
keep on adding to my collection. It's good to know I can sell it one day if I'm
short on funds. I'd also like to make them myself and I'm looking for someone
who can teach me – I have lots of ideas but none of the right skills.

[pause]

Now you will hear Part Three again.

tone

[The recording is repeated.]

[pause]

That is the end of Part Three.

Now turn to Part Four.

[pause]

PART 4   *You will hear an interview with a scientist called Peter Crane, who is talking about an ancient tree called the gingko. For questions 24 to 30, choose the best answer (A, B or C).*

You now have one minute to look at Part Four.

[pause]

tone

Interviewer: Thank you for coming into our studio today, Peter, to tell us about your research into an ancient species of tree called the gingko. First of all, how did you develop an interest in it?

Peter: I think that anyone who's seriously interested in plants inevitably comes across the gingko tree pretty early in their training, because very unusually, it's a single plant species with no known living relatives; what particularly fascinated me was the fact that it's been essentially unchanged for more than two hundred million years. Other people are attracted by its distinctive leaf – once you see it, you don't forget it.

Interviewer: When was the gingko first cultivated?

Peter: Our best estimate is about one thousand years ago in China, which is somewhat late. There's a lot of Chinese literature from before that time, and it doesn't mention the gingko, while it does mention a lot of other plants. The evidence points to the fact that the gingko was probably always a rather rare tree, until it first attracted the attention of people about a thousand years ago, when they realised it could be cultivated as a source of nuts.

Interviewer: And does the gingko tree have medical uses?

Peter: The plant itself has long been valued for its healing properties. The medicinal uses in the East and the West have gone in different directions, using two different parts of the plant: mainly the seeds in the East, and mainly the leaves in the West. In the West, work has been done on the leaves to see whether they contain substances that might help improve people's memories. The results, however, have shown no strong evidence for such powers.

Interviewer: What else do humans use the gingko tree for?

Peter: Well, it's a very popular tree in city streets all over the world. It's incredibly tough, so can tolerate conditions that might kill other types of tree. It's hard to know exactly why, but the leaves are particularly unattractive to insects that harm other trees. And it seems to survive in a street setting: its roots aren't getting much oxygen, they're getting a lot of salt and goodness knows what else is getting poured on them, but it seems relatively resistant to that.

Interviewer: You're interested in the benefits of street trees in general, aren't you, Peter?

Peter: That's right, I am. They're important for a number of reasons. One advantage is that trees along a street make it feel narrower and cause drivers to go more slowly. And obviously they provide shade, making people feel a lot more comfortable; they don't mind being outside if they can be in the shade. And so trees help bring all the benefits that come from that: kids playing outside, neighbours keeping an eye on each other's houses, people encouraged to linger in a shopping area that they would otherwise walk right through.

Interviewer: Do you think there are lessons we can learn from the gingko about preserving other plant species?

Peter: Well, because humans have distributed gingko around the planet, they have helped ensure the species' long-term survival. There are probably a couple of wild original populations of gingko tree still left in China, but even those may have been aided by people. Obviously, we should try to preserve animals and plants in their native habitats, but in the same way that we've used other methods for conserving large mammals, I think conservation through widespread cultivation is essential for preserving plant diversity for the future.

Interviewer: And finally, does working on such an ancient tree species affect your view of the world?

Peter: Yes, as humans, one of our biggest shortcomings is that we can't see the long term. So reflecting on a plant like gingko that was around in very different ecosystems hundreds of millions of years ago, really makes our own species seem very young.

[pause]

Now you will hear Part Four again.

[Teacher, repeat the track now.]

[pause]

That is the end of Part Four.

There will now be a pause of five minutes for you to copy your answers onto the separate answer sheet. Be sure to follow the numbering of all the questions. I shall remind you when there is one minute left, so that you are sure to finish in time.

That is the end of the test. Please stop now. Your supervisor will now collect all the question papers and answer sheets.

Test 7 Key

Reading and Use of English (1 hour 15 minutes)

Part 1

1 C   2 B   3 A   4 B   5 A   6 C   7 D   8 D

Part 2

9 such   10 which   11 it   12 as   13 be   14 only   15 a   16 much

Part 3

17 evidence   18 twice   19 surroundings   20 Surprisingly   21 rating(s)
22 psychologist   23 significant   24 encourage

Part 4

25 WHETHER I | wanted to see
26 n't/not as | LONG as
27 has/had GONE up | (by) more
28 ONLY does | he sing
29 BENEFIT from | living OR get/gain some BENEFIT | from living
30 not getting | in TOUCH with

Part 5

31 B   32 C   33 B   34 D   35 A   36 C

Part 6

37 F   38 G   39 A   40 E   41 B   42 D

Part 7

43 C   44 E   45 B   46 D   47 E   48 B   49 D   50 C   51 A   52 C

Writing (1 hour 20 minutes)

Candidate responses are marked using the assessment scale on pages 107–108.

Listening (approximately 40 minutes)

Part 1

1 A   2 C   3 C   4 A   5 B   6 B   7 A   8 A

Part 2

9 plastic   10 rules   11 field   12 stand   13 shoulders   14 tree   15 view
16 TV / television series   17 scoring / keeping (a) score   18 parents

Part 3

19 E   20 H   21 C   22 F   23 B

Part 4

24 A   25 A   26 C   27 B   28 B   29 A   30 A

Transcript   *This is the Cambridge English: First Listening Test. Test Seven.*

I am going to give you the instructions for this test. I shall introduce each part of the test and give you time to look at the questions. At the start of each piece you will hear this sound:

tone

You will hear each piece twice.

Remember, while you are listening, write your answers on the question paper. You will have five minutes at the end of the test to copy your answers onto the separate answer sheet.

There will now be a pause. Please ask any questions now, because you must not speak during the test.

[pause]

Now open your question paper and look at Part One.

[pause]

PART 1   *You will hear people talking in eight different situations. For questions 1 to 8, choose the best answer (A, B or C).*

Question 1   *You hear two friends talking about a laptop computer.*

[pause]

tone

Man: That's a cool computer, is it new?

Woman: I bought it a while back, actually – best thing I ever did!

Man: It does look good, but I like the one I have now.

Woman: Yeah, maybe, but if you had one like mine, after twenty-four hours I swear you'd never want to go back to your old one!

Man: Really? Why's that?

Woman: Well, there are just so many fantastic features – I'd let you borrow it, but I just can't live without it!

Man: It must have been expensive, though …

Woman: Not really, considering how much it can do.

[pause]

tone

[The recording is repeated.]

[pause]

Question 2   *You hear two students talking about a play they have just seen.*

[pause]

tone

Man: That was good, wasn't it?

Woman: Not bad – I wasn't sure about the script, though – I'm not sure people ever really spoke like that, even in those days!

Man: Yeah, you may be right there, but the actors coped with it, didn't they? They were pretty convincing, I thought.

Woman: They had poor material to work with, but I'm with you on that – I don't think anyone could have done better.

Man: And the set design was unusual, wasn't it?

Woman: Just a bit too unusual for me, I'm afraid. I think something more traditional would have been less distracting.

Man: Yeah, maybe you're right …

[pause]

tone

[The recording is repeated.]

[pause]

Question 3   *You hear two people talking about a friend.*

[pause]

tone

Man: I saw Mike the other day.

Woman: Oh, how was he?

Man: Seems to be enjoying his new job.

Woman: Oh good. He never has trouble making new friends, does he?

Man: Well … he doesn't really talk much about himself until you get to know him.

Woman: I suppose. But he's very easy-going – whatever goes wrong in his life, he seems to stay cheerful.

Man: Well that's true … nothing much seems to upset him, does it?

Woman: But I'm not sure the new job is really him. He'd be better off long term in a job where he can help others.

Man: Only time will tell. He needs to give it a try.

[pause]

tone

[The recording is repeated.]

[pause]

Question 4   *You hear a lecturer talking to some of his students about their history project.*

[pause]

tone

Well the deadline's not for a while yet, so there's plenty of time for you to choose your topic for your nineteenth-century history project and read up on it. There's been a lot written on this period that you'll find useful I'm sure. Books are a great source of information, as well as the internet of course – but check your facts carefully and use reliable websites. Also make sure you come and see me if there's anything that's unclear or you think I can help you with. Straight after a lecture is a good time to catch me. And finally, good luck, everybody!

[pause]

tone

[The recording is repeated.]

[pause]

Question 5   *You hear two TV sports presenters talking about their work.*

[pause]

tone

Man: We started off by covering the swimming championships together last year, didn't we? And I reckon that helped us build an essential rapport with each other and the viewers. Presenting's not something you can learn, though. It has to be natural, like adopting a suitably sympathetic expression when you're announcing disappointing results.

Woman: Well, I'd say presenters do best when they're making it look fun and spontaneous, even if they're actually sticking to a script. Nobody likes seeing presenters who aren't having a good time. And they need to have that connection with whoever's watching.

Man: And the relevant subject knowledge always helps too.

Woman: You're right.

[pause]

tone

[The recording is repeated.]

[pause]

Question 6   *You hear a woman talking about a radio programme.*

[pause]

tone

Well it's a programme that's on every week, about the countryside. It can get a little boring, but I listen to it anyway, as I always have the radio on when I'm driving home from work. I was curious when they started talking about a village, because it all sounded rather familiar. And then I realised they were talking about somewhere I'd been to on a family holiday as a child. I turned the volume up then, because I didn't want to miss a word of it – not because I didn't know quite a lot about the village already. I just wanted to know what they thought about it.

[pause]

tone

[The recording is repeated.]

[pause]

Question 7   *You hear two music students talking about an assignment they have to do.*

[pause]

tone

Woman: That talk about next year's assignment was good, but I'm not sure I understood everything. I liked the sound of having to perform a song or instrumental piece and record it in the studio.

Man: … And you can get help from your team – thank goodness! The technical side's not my strong point!

Woman: But then there was something about a commentary.

Man: Yes, you have to write a long commentary on it, saying how you organised everything and how you overcame difficulties.

Woman: But are we supposed to also say how we think it went … you know, analyse our own performance?

Man: Hmm … I can ask my sister – she did it two years ago.

[pause]

tone

[The recording is repeated.]

[pause]

Question 8   *You hear a writer talking about a book she wrote which has been turned into a film.*

[pause]

tone

Of course, it's wonderful when your book is made into a film or a TV series. It's the greatest compliment, but the hardest thing for a writer is handing your book over to someone else and letting their ideas take over. I've done it four times now and it doesn't get any easier. When I met the current director I thought we'd be working together, but he listened to my views of how the film should be made, then completely ignored them! Despite that though, he's done my writing justice and I'm glad he didn't listen to me.

[pause]

tone

[The recording is repeated.]

[pause]

That is the end of Part One.

Now turn to Part Two.

[pause]

PART 2

You will hear a woman called Anne Ruskin giving a talk about a one-day archery course, during which she learnt to use a bow to shoot arrows at a target. For questions 9 to 18, complete the sentences with a word or short phrase.

You now have forty-five seconds to look at Part Two.

[pause]

tone

Hello, my name's Anne Ruskin. Thank you very much for inviting me to your college this evening to talk about my experiences on a one-day archery course.

When you were little, I imagine many of you, like me, used to have bows and shoot arrows from them – wooden bows you made from branches or maybe a plastic one like mine. Lots of kids love them – I even saw a little metal set in a toyshop the other day.

Anyway, I decided that now I was an adult I'd have a go at the real thing, and signed up for a beginners' archery course. I had planned to read up a bit on the history of archery beforehand, not knowing much about it. But I ran out of time and only managed a quick scan through the rules. I've found out more about it since, and it's fascinating.

The archery courses are generally held in a variety of locations, depending on the season and the weather. In winter, they even use a large gym if the weather's really bad. I was happy that mine was in the field they use in the summer, though I suppose a medieval castle or some woods would be the ideal setting.

There was so much to learn, I really had to concentrate. It was far harder than I'd imagined to stand in the right way, but how to hold the bow correctly came to me relatively quickly. I was also taught to place the arrows in exactly the right position in the bow.

Soon most of my body was aching! The teacher showed me some exercises to strengthen my hands, so I'll be able to grip the bow tightly for longer. He told me my shoulders were too tense and reassured me that my arms would eventually become stronger if I practised enough. I hope he's right!

Perhaps due to beginner's luck, most of my arrows went in the right direction, and into the target, though I never managed to hit the middle! And I did manage to hit a tree, narrowly missing a bench and a bag I'd left underneath it! That certainly wasn't deliberate! Someone else hit the target next to theirs instead of their own!

There were regular breaks, and part of the appeal of archery is the delightfully calm rhythm. There was a lot of time to drink tea, and enjoy the view, and I did plenty of both. There were some archery books and photographs to look through showing us how we could improve, and some people took the opportunity to check their phones for messages, but I preferred to chat.

I asked some of the other people there why they had decided to do the course. In fact, I'd imagined it might be because of a website or something. In fact, it turned out to be because of a TV series. The archery courses are advertised on local radio too, but none of us had actually heard about them that way.

The teacher made sure we practised loads of shooting and it was thrilling when he finally let us do some scoring. There are rings on the targets, and you get points depending on where your arrow lands. It was fun to see how well I was doing compared to everyone else! And I must say, I wasn't too bad!

I loved it, and archery is one of those rare sports that almost anyone can do, including children, though they must be over the age of ten. Some of my friends have said they'll join me next time I go, and I'm working on my parents at the moment, in the hope that they'll come along as well.

Thank you all for listening. I hope some of you will consider taking archery up. It really is a great leisure activity. Now, have any of you got any questions? I'd be happy to tell you more about … [fade]

[pause]

Now you will hear Part Two again.

[Teacher, repeat the track now.]

[pause]

That is the end of Part Two.

Now turn to Part Three.

[pause]

PART 3

You will hear five short extracts in which people are talking about when they moved their office from one building to another. For questions 19 to 23, choose from the list (A to H) what each speaker says. Use the letters only once. There are three extra letters which you do not need to use.

You now have thirty seconds to look at Part Three.

[pause]

tone

Speaker 1

We decided to move our office from the centre of London to a town about thirty kilometres away. Our office in the centre of London was very expensive to run and we knew we'd make a lot of money from selling the building because it was in an excellent location. The administrative staff decided to resign because they enjoyed working in London and didn't want to move. We had to accept that, but we had to dissuade our top managers from leaving, so some of the money we got from selling the building was given to them in the form of a bonus.

[pause]

Speaker 2

Our company decided to move office at what would be a very busy time of year for our department. So a number of us in the department tried to get the date changed so that our work wouldn't suffer. No luck with that, but at least senior management were aware of the problems we would have. I knew that everywhere would be in chaos on the day itself, so I collected as many empty boxes from the removal company as I could and was glad that I did, because in the end they came in handy for me to pack my stuff in.

[pause]

Speaker 3

About three years ago we moved our office from one side of the street to another. First of all, we set up a small group of people to be in charge of the move and any requests had to go through them. That made everything more organised and democratic. However, quite a few things still went missing during the move. For instance, we couldn't find the computer manager's cupboard and eventually it turned up in our old building. OK, these things happen, but when you use a well-established company to do your move, you expect better.

[pause]

Speaker 4

Moving offices always creates disruption, so we said, why not use this opportunity to reorganise where people sit. The offices are now arranged according to people's responsibilities. So staff in each office can work together without having to phone one another. There were things we didn't take into consideration though, like the size of the canteen, which turned out to be much too small. Moving to new offices is like moving house; many of the problems are the same.

[pause]

Speaker 5

Always bear in mind the amount of thinking ahead that you're going to need when you move. We took a few little things like the files we were working on at the time and our personal belongings, but we failed to give the removal company clear enough instructions about the rest. We couldn't find several important invoices we needed to access, because they'd put them in the wrong room. We resolved not to follow it up, though, as it wasn't really their fault. We found we needed at least two days; one to clear everything out, and the other to set it all up in the new offices. And then we spent months trying to find out where everything was.

[pause]

Now you will hear Part Three again.

tone

[The recording is repeated.]

[pause]

That is the end of Part Three.

Now turn to Part Four.

[pause]

PART 4 *You will hear part of a radio interview with someone called Jane Brown, who is a home economist working in the food industry. For questions 24 to 30, choose the best answer (A, B or C).*

You now have one minute to look at Part Four.

[pause]

tone

Interviewer: In our series of interviews about people's jobs, we're delighted to welcome Jane Brown, who works in the food industry.

Jane: Hi!

Interviewer: Now I know you studied home economics at Longley University, Jane. Why did you go there?

Jane: Well some of my friends also studied home economics, and they wanted me to go to the same university as them rather than to Longley. If I'd done that, I could have shared a flat with them – that would've been fun but being closer to home really appealed to me and made getting used to being a student that bit easier.

Interviewer: And did you enjoy the course?

Jane: I loved it! I've always been interested in food chemistry, so that's what I specialised in. The class sizes were small so the staff knew us all by name and all about us. I'd always enjoyed working with other people, and I did a lot of that on the course. The university also made sure we had plenty of opportunities to get out of the classroom and apply things we'd learnt in theory to real life.

Interviewer: I suppose you also learned about things like food tasting?

Jane: A group of us would all have to taste the same dish and try to decide if the general public would like it. As the training got more complex it became harder to agree, and there were even conflicts and tense moments. We had really long arguments about flavours, but it was worth it in the end.

Interviewer: And what was your first job after university?

Jane: I worked for a large food company, in the sauces team, testing out new recipes and making sure the quality of the sauces they produced was consistent. When I applied, I knew I could do it, and it was really a step along the way to something more interesting. But there were a lot of applicants and the food industry isn't always an easy one to get into, so I was very aware of how lucky I was.

Interviewer: Is there anything you particularly remember about that first job?

Jane: Yes, I assisted in the development of a new product, a delicious cheese sauce! It was very different at first to be making decisions on my own and doing things without the support of the people I'd studied with for three years, but I coped pretty well, I think. The team I was in managed to reduce the salt content of the cheese sauce while keeping it tasty, which wasn't straightforward. And then of course it was great to see it on supermarket shelves!

Interviewer: Yeah, it must have been exciting! So what did you do next?

Jane: Well that first company sent me to work in Denmark for two years. That was really interesting. Part of my job involved visiting local food companies, and that way I met lots of people I'm still in touch with who've helped me and taught me loads. And on a personal level, it was great to discover a new country and culture, as well as a whole new food culture.

Interviewer: Out of all the different things you mentioned Jane, there must be some things you enjoy more than others?

Jane: There are lots of different things I have to do. For example I have to interview clients, to find out about and understand what they need; I taste food to assess its quality – rather a lot of that, which actually isn't always that great when the food gets really unusual! And then there are reports to write, which some people hate but I never mind. And lots of other things too, so every day is different. I really think I have a fantastic job and would certainly recommend it to anyone who's interested in food and how it's produced.

Interviewer: Thanks very much, Jane, that's been really interesting … [fade]

[pause]

Now you will hear Part Four again.

[Teacher, repeat the track now.]

[pause]

That is the end of Part Four.

There will now be a pause of five minutes for you to copy your answers onto the separate answer sheet. Be sure to follow the numbering of all the questions. I shall remind you when there is one minute left, so that you are sure to finish in time.

That is the end of the test. Please stop now. Your supervisor will now collect all the question papers and answer sheets.

Test 8 Key

Reading and Use of English (1 hour 15 minutes)

Part 1

1 A   2 D   3 B   4 D   5 C   6 D   7 B   8 C

Part 2

9 as   10 for   11 more   12 were   13 no   14 what   15 who/that
16 well

Part 3

17 decision   18 unfortunately   19 vacancy   20 commitment
21 enthusiastic   22 variety   23 daily   24 spectacular

Part 4

25 TAKE his | clothes off OR TAKE off | his clothes
26 was RESPONSIBLE | for ringing/calling/(tele)phoning
27 not/n't AS | enjoyable AS
28 in COMING | up with OR in COMING | to
29 WISHES she had not / hadn't | bought
30 on ACCOUNT of | missing

Part 5

31 C   32 D   33 B   34 B   35 A   36 A

Part 6

37 F   38 E   39 A   40 G   41 D   42 B

Part 7

43 D   44 B   45 D   46 C   47 A   48 D   49 D
50 C   51 A   52 D

Writing (1 hour 20 minutes)

Candidate responses are marked using the assessment scale on pages 107–108.

Listening (approximately 40 minutes)

Part 1

1 C   2 C   3 A   4 C   5 B   6 A   7 A   8 B

Part 2

9 engineer   10 skis   11 loneliness/lonelyness   12 water   13 weight   14 toes
15 rest   16 half(-)way   17 relief   18 alien

Part 3

19 E   20 H   21 A   22 C   23 F

Part 4

24 B   25 B   26 A   27 C   28 A   29 B   30 A

Transcript   *This is the Cambridge English: First Listening Test. Test Eight.*

I am going to give you the instructions for this test. I shall introduce each part of the test and give you time to look at the questions. At the start of each piece you will hear this sound:

tone

You will hear each piece twice.

Remember, while you are listening, write your answers on the question paper. You will have five minutes at the end of the test to copy your answers onto the separate answer sheet.

There will now be a pause. Please ask any questions now, because you must not speak during the test.

[pause]

Now open your question paper and look at Part One.

[pause]

PART 1 | *You will hear people talking in eight different situations. For questions 1 to 8, choose the best answer (A, B or C).*

Question 1 | *You hear two people talking about some music they're listening to.*

[pause]

tone

Man: Oh, I love this song by The Foolz!

Woman: Do you? I find it a bit sad.

Man: Yeah, I know what you mean. I do normally like music that's a bit more light-hearted, but this particular one still works for me. My parents always played upbeat stuff by The Foolz at home, so when I first heard this track, it came as a bit of a surprise.

Woman: I can imagine – it's quite different from their usual style.

Man: No one in my family plays a musical instrument, but I actually started teaching myself the guitar because I wanted to be able to play this.

Woman: And can you?

Man: Not yet! I'll be really pleased when I can!

[pause]

tone

[The recording is repeated.]

[pause]

Question 2 | *You hear part of a radio programme in which a teacher is talking about her own education.*

[pause]

tone

I was educated in quite a posh and rather expensive school, really, so expectations for pupils were high, and that put us under pressure a bit. Mind you, I wouldn't have got down to it and done much otherwise, and certainly wouldn't have gone to university. Perhaps that's why I've found my niche in trying to make sure that everyone gets the kind of education that allows them to realise their full potential in life. Teaching wasn't my first career choice, though. I think colleagues I worked with were amazed when I made the switch from industry. But I haven't looked back since I did it.

[pause]

tone

[The recording is repeated.]

[pause]

Question 3   *You hear a woman telling a friend about a new job she has.*

[pause]

tone

Man: How are you getting on with your new job in the café?

Woman: Overall enjoying it a lot. The owners are a husband and wife, and he does the cooking downstairs while she's in charge in the café. At times they're quite casual and laid back, and at others they get really stressed out, like when you make a mistake or when it gets really full at lunch time! They seem to think I'm a master of all trades and that I know how to repair their faulty coffee machine … which is much too technical for me! Anyway, I mustn't grumble … at least the customers have been nice so far, with a few exceptions who were just rather fussy for my liking.

[pause]

tone

[The recording is repeated.]

[pause]

Question 4   *You hear two students talking about an architecture course.*

[pause]

tone

Man: I'm so glad I chose architecture, aren't you?

Woman: Yeah. The course is great, but sometimes I feel I can't keep up. We always have so much work to do!

Man: I think it's about right, personally. And anyway, the teachers explain everything brilliantly!

Woman: I don't think I've ever learnt so much in such a short time, and it *is* because of them, that's true.

Man: What do you think of the other students? Some of them have fantastic ideas, don't they!

Woman: They produce good work, because they're on such an inspiring course. I'm not sure how they'd perform in a different environment, though.

Man: Yeah, you may be right. Anyway, I'm very happy.

[pause]

tone

[The recording is repeated.]

[pause]

Question 5	*You hear two students talking about the chemistry laboratories at their college.*

[pause]

tone

Man:	Did you know they're going to do up the chemistry labs next month?
Woman:	No, I didn't. Bit weird, isn't it? I mean some work was done on them last year and they're OK, I think.
Man:	Well I still think they could do with a coat of paint.
Woman:	The main thing, I'd say, is that there are just so many of us wanting to use them this year and they're too crowded.
Man:	Yeah, true, and I also think they should replace some of the equipment, don't you?
Woman:	A lot of what they have is pretty much state-of-the-art, so I wouldn't say that's much of a problem.
Man:	Maybe you're right.

[pause]

tone

[The recording is repeated.]

[pause]

Question 6   *You hear a woman talking about a place she used to visit as a child.*

[pause]

tone

Bradworth is a small seaside town and visits there were a huge part of my childhood. I have many fond memories of sailing off the coast, watching the seals, walking barefoot in the beautiful white sand and having sand fights with the other children. I remember all the parents getting together for picnics too. I've had lots of exotic vacations since then in the most amazing places but nothing to compare with those childhood memories. I'd love to go back but it wouldn't be the same any more and I'd rather hang on to those wonderful childhood memories.

[pause]

tone

[The recording is repeated.]

[pause]

Question 7   *You hear a runner telling his friend about a sports injury he has.*

[pause]

tone

Man: So the injury's making slow progress, I'm afraid.

Woman: Oh dear.

Man: Yes. I went back to the doctor, and my lower leg is still swollen. The strange thing is, apparently it actually needs a bit of exercise in order to get the blood flowing to it so that it can heal. So things like swimming and cycling are fine, although even with those I shouldn't push it … but even a bit of running is OK provided I run on soft surfaces. Then I've also been given some particular movements to do in front of a mirror which will stimulate the injured area in the right way.

[pause]

tone

[The recording is repeated.]

[pause]

Question 8   *You hear a woman talking about her favourite radio programme.*

[pause]

tone

I listen to a lot of stuff on the radio and I love hearing about stories of normal people leading normal lives. For several years now, I've been really into a programme called 'Your Turn' where people basically tell a story from their own life. Sometimes these stories can be quite gripping and emotional and at other times they can pass you by, but anyway I love having it on in the background while I'm working. It's a really clever idea actually. The stories have to be true and they're told – not read, but told – and they're delivered in front of a live audience. Really effective.

[pause]

tone

[The recording is repeated.]

[pause]

That is the end of Part One.

Now turn to Part Two.

[pause]

PART 2 *You will hear a man called Peter Green talking about a group expedition he went on to the South Pole for a TV documentary. For questions 9 to 18, complete the sentences with a word or short phrase.*

You now have forty-five seconds to look at Part Two.

[pause]

tone

Hi, my name's Peter and I'm going to talk about how I ended up in a TV documentary about going to the South Pole. Basically, what happened was, I spotted an online advert asking for people to apply for the trip of a lifetime. A TV company was making a documentary programme about this, and had left one place on the expedition for a member of the public to take part. I applied as, in my work as an engineer, I'd worked with an environmentalist who'd really inspired me with his tales of the South Pole. To my great surprise, I was accepted.

The TV company were keen to make the documentary unusual … for example concerning the transport. The idea was that we'd travel on skis, rather than using dogs and sledges, as many people have done before us.

In fact, the expedition turned out to be much, much harder than I ever thought it would be. Before I went, I thought the most challenging thing would be the physical toll on my body. And yes, it was incredibly challenging. But even though I wasn't alone – there were five others in the group – it was the loneliness I found the hardest to take. I really missed my family and friends, especially my wife.

The Antarctic trip took us seven weeks in all and we were travelling across an icy wilderness in sub-zero temperatures. We kept going for up to sixteen hours a day and we burnt nine thousand calories each and every day. It was crucial that those calories were replaced but our main preoccupation was the constant need to make water from the snow so we didn't become dehydrated.

We carried snack-packs of high-calorie food like cheese, salami, nuts and chocolate, and we cooked dehydrated meals with loads of fat for breakfast and dinner. It was incredible that fairly soon into the journey I'd lost the weight I had deliberately put on before I started. Despite this, I didn't suffer loss of concentration or motivation.

However, by the time we reached the South Pole I was beginning to suffer from exhaustion, and I was afraid that my toes would be permanently damaged by the freezing temperatures. Luckily the special gloves I wore saved my fingers from having the same problem.

My team-mates suffered too. Of course, we all found the temperature difficult to take, but one of our group, John, suffered the most health problems. He developed a chest infection and the altitude didn't help that at all – neither did the fact that we rarely had a rest, because we needed to keep walking. This took us all by surprise, as John had been the fittest and most well-prepared member of the team before we started.

At various points on the journey we had breaks. At the halfway point we were examined by doctors and John was nearly forbidden from continuing. He was only given permission to carry on at the last minute. If he hadn't been allowed to carry on, that would have been the end of the whole adventure.

Lots of people have asked me why I went. It's a difficult question to answer. When I was travelling, all I could think about was getting through each day, and then when we got to the South Pole, rather than feeling a sense of achievement, I actually felt relief. It was an amazing experience. It's so incredible when you think that we survived for so long in such a physically and mentally demanding environment, which I can only call 'alien'. I don't think I'll want to go back there for quite some time!

[pause]

Now you will hear Part Two again.

[Teacher, repeat the track now.]

[pause]

That is the end of Part Two.

Now turn to Part Three.

[pause]

PART 3   *You will hear five short extracts in which people are talking about how to give good presentations. For questions 19 to 23, choose from the list (A to H) what advice each person gives. Use the letters only once. There are three extra letters which you do not need to use.*

You now have thirty seconds to look at Part Three.

[pause]

tone

Speaker 1

I haven't given many presentations so far, but I have talked to a lot of my fellow students about them and I'm certainly more relaxed about giving them than I used to be. The main thing as far as I'm concerned is to make sure you've already given it loads of times before you're actually standing in front of your audience. You may risk boring yourself to tears, but believe me, it's worth it! And I don't mean you should give a shorter version, either. They need to hear every single word, from start to finish. The best people to help you with this are your friends and family.

[pause]

Speaker 2

When you're planning your presentation, the main point to remember is laughably simple: you're trying to communicate something to other people, so the focus has to be on them, not on you. That means the more you know about them, the better. I can remember one of my college lecturers repeating this time and again, and I think she was absolutely right. However well you know your subject and however many jokes you tell, your presentation won't be a success unless you bear this point in mind. There's a big difference between a talk for people who already know a lot about a subject and one for those who don't.

[pause]

Speaker 3

In my opinion, a good presentation isn't necessarily one which makes the audience laugh, or one that has wonderful graphics to illustrate the speaker's points. The key thing, I'd say, is to make sure you hold your audience's attention throughout, and you'll only be able to do that if you don't go on at length. That may sound easy, but if you're too relaxed you're in danger of forgetting this basic rule. When you're preparing, it's important to decide what your main message is and work out how best to communicate it briefly. If you can do that there'll be no need to repeat the same point three times.

[pause]

Speaker 4

Many people think that to give a good presentation, you need to practise a lot, but I find that just makes me nervous for days in advance. I think audiences need something to focus on while they're listening. Colour diagrams and graphs are a really engaging way of putting your message across, and everyone will enjoy your input more, including you. If you're short of ideas however, try to avoid telling jokes, which are no substitute for the real thing, that is, information. And you can always ask your fellow students and colleagues about what materials they've used in the past!

[pause]

Speaker 5

If you're well prepared and know what you're talking about, then your presentation should be a pleasure to give as well as to listen to. If you feel comfortable and can manage to look as if you're enjoying yourself, then the audience will respond to this and enjoy your presentation more. I'm not saying it'll be easy at first, but the more you give different presentations, the easier you'll find it. When I had to speak to a very large audience for the first time, I pictured them all sitting in trees wearing silly hats. It's probably best, though, to focus on your subject matter rather than on the audience!

[pause]

Now you will hear Part Three again.

tone

[The recording is repeated.]

[pause]

That is the end of Part Three.

Now turn to Part Four.

[pause]

PART 4   *You will hear an interview with a woman called Maggie Wharton who is skilled in the sport of kitesurfing. For questions 24 to 30, choose the best answer (A, B or C).*

You now have one minute to look at Part Four.

[pause]

tone

Interviewer: So Maggie, welcome to the studio. Tell us about the sport of kitesurfing. What is it and how did you get into it?

Maggie: Well, in kitesurfing your feet are strapped to a surfboard and you're holding on to a big kite – and the wind takes you along on the water at tremendous speed. From the point when I started, a long time ago, it took me about a year to feel I could really call myself a kitesurfer. At least I was physically in good enough shape from the outset, though the lack of any really suitable instruction obstructed my progress. Having said that, it was straightforward to get everything you needed, but there wasn't the range you see now – it's become one of the fastest-growing sports in the country.

Interviewer: So what's changed in the sport during that time?

Maggie: Well, helmets have gained increasing popularity, and I guess they're good, because if you fall off you could easily hit your head, but my generation never felt the need for one. On the other hand, the wind is the fundamental element that all kitesurfers have to learn about. For example, you should never go on the water if the wind's coming from off the land as you could be blown out to sea – and I'm not sure if kitesurfers now are as up on that as we were. Of course, they'll know obvious things like not surfing in places near rocks or power lines – but sadly those hazards still aren't as flagged up as they might be.

Interviewer: Right – and you now take part in international events.

Maggie: Yes, I'm going to Fiji soon for an eight-day competition. It's a new event but the organisers are keen to get it as a regular fixture on the calendar. We'll cover a hundred and fifty kilometres and perhaps a new world record'll be set in distance kitesurfing. And it'll be great if, as a result of seeing me take part, people will decide to give it a go. But it's not just distance, we'll be able to show off some freestyle tricks, too.

Interviewer: But you've done some amazing distance events before.

Maggie: Yeah, I've kitesurfed well over a hundred kilometres. That was tough – particularly on the feet and knees. And the fog meant my support boat was no longer visible for a while, which was an uncomfortable feeling. Then halfway across, I changed to a bigger kite so I could get more speed, and things went more smoothly after that. But apart from a few dolphins for company, we were out in the middle of the sea alone.

Interviewer: An amazing achievement! So why've you done so well, do you think?

Maggie: Well, it was always likely that I'd take up some kind of water sport because I grew up near the sea and my parents taught me to swim at an early age. It was the unpredictability of kitesurfing that appealed to my nature, really – I've always gone for things that are less straightforward. But of course, you don't get anywhere if you don't practise.

Interviewer: And kitesurfing's a growing sport. What do you think about the people taking it up now?

Maggie: Well, kitesurfing's a free-and-easy sport without many regulations that everyone has to follow. But, having said that, I've met a number of new people who are attracted to the sport because of the stuff you do up in the air, rather than on the water. What they don't realise is that the dos and don'ts of the sport have to be mastered before they try something so ambitious – they're too impatient – although one day they may well achieve great things once they've grasped those.

Interviewer: What is there left for you to do in the sport?

Maggie: Enjoy it, mostly – I'll leave the competition for the young guys. But I still need to set myself goals, and I'm keen to help bring a bit more sponsorship into the sport without making it too commercial. My partner's also a kitesurfer – he teaches young kids in the local area, and I help him. So I might even do more of that one day – who knows?

Interviewer: Maggie, thanks … [fade]

[pause]

Now you will hear Part Four again.

[Teacher, repeat the track now.]

[pause]

That is the end of Part Four.

There will now be a pause of five minutes for you to copy your answers onto the separate answer sheet. Be sure to follow the numbering of all the questions. I shall remind you when there is one minute left, so that you are sure to finish in time.

That is the end of the test. Please stop now. Your supervisor will now collect all the question papers and answer sheets.

Sample answer sheet: Reading and Use of English

CAMBRIDGE ENGLISH
Language Assessment
Part of the University of Cambridge

Do not write in this box

SAMPLE

Candidate Name
If not already printed, write name
in CAPITALS and complete the
Candidate No. grid (in pencil).

Candidate Signature

Examination Title

Centre

Supervisor:
If the candidate is ABSENT or has WITHDRAWN shade here

Centre No.

Candidate No.

Examination Details

Candidate Answer Sheet

Instructions

Use a PENCIL (B or HB).

Rub out any answer you wish
to change using an eraser.

Parts 1, 5, 6 and **7:**
Mark ONE letter for each
question.

For example, if you think **B** is the right
answer to the question, mark your
answer sheet like this:

Parts 2, 3 and **4:**
Write your answer clearly
in CAPITAL LETTERS.

For Parts 2 and 3 write one letter
in each box. For example:

Part 1

1	A	B	C	D
2	A	B	C	D
3	A	B	C	D
4	A	B	C	D
5	A	B	C	D
6	A	B	C	D
7	A	B	C	D
8	A	B	C	D

Part 2

Do not write
below here

9		1 0 u
10		1 0 u
11		1 0 u
12		1 0 u
13		1 0 u
14		1 0 u
15		1 0 u
16		1 0 u

Continues over ➡

FCE R

DP802

© UCLES 2016 Photocopiable

168

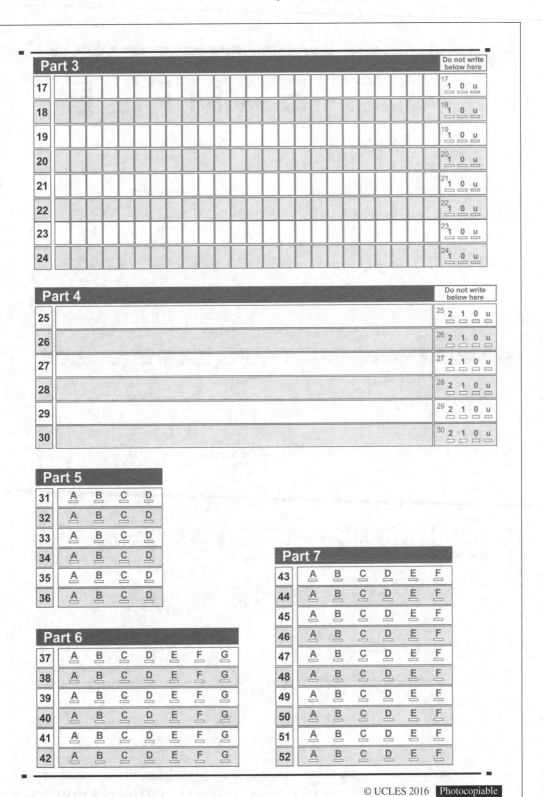

Sample answer sheet: Listening

CAMBRIDGE ENGLISH
Language Assessment
Part of the University of Cambridge

Do not write in this box

SAMPLE

Candidate Name
If not already printed, write name
in CAPITALS and complete the
Candidate No. grid (in pencil).

Candidate Signature

Examination Title

Centre

Supervisor:
If the candidate is ABSENT or has WITHDRAWN shade here ▭

Centre No.

Candidate No.

Examination
Details

0	0	0	0
1	1	1	1
2	2	2	2
3	3	3	3
4	4	4	4
5	5	5	5
6	6	6	6
7	7	7	7
8	8	8	8
9	9	9	9

—

=

—

Candidate Answer Sheet

Instructions

Use a PENCIL (B or HB).
Rub out any answer you wish to change using an eraser.

Parts 1, 3 and 4:
Mark ONE letter for each question.

For example, if you think **B** is the
right answer to the question, mark
your answer sheet like this:

Part 2:
Write your answer clearly in CAPITAL LETTERS.

Write one letter or number in each box.
If the answer has more than one word, leave one
box empty between words.

For example:

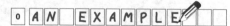

Turn this sheet over to start.

© UCLES 2016 Photocopiable

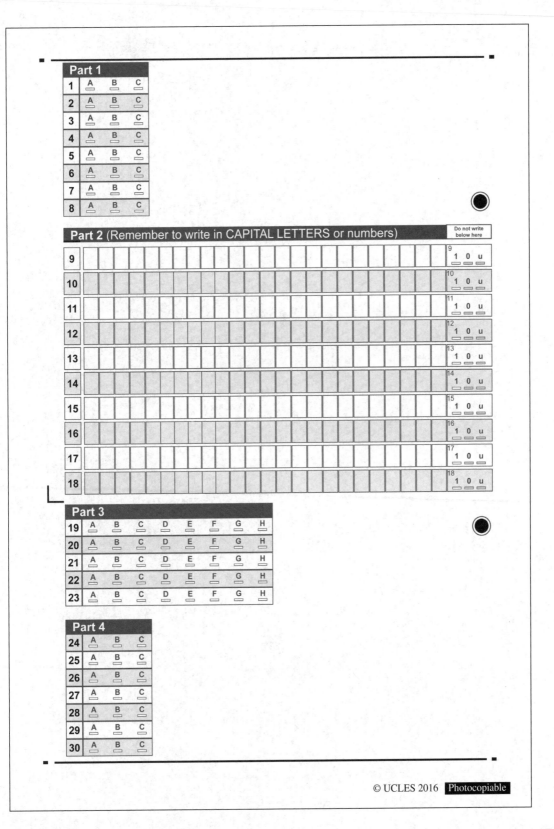

© UCLES 2016 Photocopiable

Thanks and acknowledgements

The authors and publishers acknowledge the following sources of copyright material and are grateful for the permissions granted. While every effort has been made, it has not always been possible to identify the sources of all the material used, or to trace all copyright holders. If any omissions are brought to our notice, we will be happy to include the appropriate acknowledgements on reprinting and in the next update to the digital edition, as applicable.

Text acknowledgements

Text on p. 10 adapted from "Extraordinary Cats – Homing Instinct". Copyright © 2016 WNET. Reproduced with permission of WNET; Text on p. 11 adapted from 'Britain's Oldest House Found in North Yorkshire' by Martin Wainwright, *The Guardian*, 10.08.10. Copyright Guardian News & Media Ltd 2015; Text on p. 14 adapted from 'Plane crazy' by Matt Rud, *The Sunday Times* 23.02.14. Copyright © Times Newspapers Ltd. Reproduced with permission of News Syndication; Text on p. 16 adapted from 'Sleep and Memory'. Copyright 2008 by the President and Fellows of Harvard College; Text on p. 19 adapted from 'Adventure guides – following the leader', *The Guardian*, 23.11.12. Copyright Guardian News & Media Ltd 2015; Text on p. 22 adapted from 'Why A-listers queue up to work with David Hare' by Ben Dowell. Copyright © Immediate Media Company Limited. Reproduced with permission; Text on p. 24 adapted from 'York Children's University broadens pupils' horizons' and 'A degree of success for York children'. Copyright © University of York. Reproduced with permission; Text on p. 25 adapted from 'Why we want to spend the rest of our lives on Mars' by Josh Davis, *The Guardian*, 19.01.2014. Copyright Guardian News & Media Ltd 2015; Text on p. 25 adapted from "Mission to colonise Mars: 'Columbus didn't wait; nor should we'" by Carmen Fishwick, *The Guardian*, 10.09.2013. Copyright Guardian News & Media Ltd 2015; Text on p. 30 adapted from 'The beating heart of science' by Ben Gilliland. Copyright © Cosmonline. Reproduced with permission; Text on p. 33 adapted from 'On my travels' by Sive O'Brien. Copyright © IMAGE Publications. Reproduced by kind permission of Sive O'Brien; Text on p. 36 adapted from 'Wildlife cameraman Doug Allan: I like to get on an animal's wavelength' by John Vidal, *The Guardian*, 08.04.14. Copyright Guardian News & Media Ltd 2015; Text on p. 38 adapted from 'Ancient Tomb Painting Provides Answer to Pyramid Building Mystery, Allegra Staples' by Allegra Staples. Copyright © DOGO Media, Inc. Reproduced with permission; Text on p. 41 adapted from Extract, (c.170w), from *Sleepfaring: A Journey Through the Science of Sleep* by Jim Horne (2007) Extract, (c.170w), from *Dreaming: An Introduction to the Science of Sleep* by J. Allan Hobson (2002). Reproduced with permission of Oxford University Press; Text on p. 41 republished with permission of KIRKUS MEDIA LLC, from KIRKUS REVIEW; permission conveyed through Copyright Clearance Center, Inc; Text on p. 46 adapted from 'My time studying the NCTJ Diploma' by Ru Barratt. Copyright © Brighton Journalist Works. Reproduced with permission; The History Press for the text on p. 52 adapted from *A Little Book of Manchester* by Stuart Hylton. Copyright © The History Press. Reproduced with permission; Text on p. 54 from 'Getting lost in a good book can help keep you healthy' by Hilary Freeman, *The Mail on Sunday* 25.08.12, Copyright © Associated Newspapers Ltd. Reproduced with permission; The Times for the text on p. 55 from 'Diners Prefer Rich Taste', *The Times* 26.09.14. Copyright © Times Newspapers Limited. Reproduced with permission of News Syndication; Robert Lilwall for the text on p. 58 from *Cycling Home from Siberia* by Robert Lilwall. Reproduced by kind permission of Robert Lilwall; Immediate Media Company Limited for the text on p. 60 adapted from 'Puffins in peril' by Mike Harris, *Discover Wildlife* 15.01.12, Copyright © Immediate Media Company Ltd. 2016; Text on p. 63 adapted from *Poetry and Precision* by Clive Gregory. Copyright © Marshall Cavendish; Text on p. 74 adapted from 'Sherlock Holmes and Dr. Joseph Bell'. Copyright ©2016 – The Chronicles of Sir Arthur Conan Doyle. Reproduced by kind permission of Marsha Perry; Text on p. 76 adapted from 'Why do we laugh?' by Jill Suttie. Copyright © The Greater Good Science Center. Reproduced with permission; Text on p. 77 adapted from 'Did you always want to be a pilot, and what do you enjoy about it? First Officer' by Chris Walther. Copyright © EasyJet Airline Company Limited. Reproduced by kind permission; The Independent for the text on p. 80 adapted from 'Pen Hadow: Because it's there ... but for how long?', *The Independent* 23.10.11. Copyright © The Independent; Jeremy Evans for the text on p. 82 adapted from *Inline Skating* Jeremy Evans. Copyright © Parragon Books Ltd. Reproduced by kind permission of Jeremy Evans; Text on p. 85 adapted from 'Saying no to marshmallows: an encounter with the sage of self-control' by Sophie McBain, *New Statesman*, 23.10.14. Copyright © New Statesman Limited; The Independent for the text on p. 134 adapted from 'Juan Diego Flórez: the best tenor in the world?' by Jessica Duchen, *The Independent* 19.03.14. Copyright © The Independent; The Independent for the text on p. 135 adapted from 'This is England, Broadchurch and now Line of Duty – how does Vicky McClure keep her feet on the ground?' by Holly Williams, *The Independent* 16.03.14. Copyright © The Independent; Text on p. 136 adapted from 'Ballet's Gillian Lynne and Beryl Grey: dancers should be pushed to the limit' by Dalya Alberge, *The Guardian*, 12.02.14. Copyright Guardian News & Media Ltd 2015; The Independent for the text on p. 136 adapted from "How we met: Valentine Warner & Nathan Outlaw – 'You really know when he's been in the kitchen, as it looks like a train wreck'" by Adam Jacques, *The Independent* 09.03.14. Copyright © The Independent; The Independent for the text on p. 148 adapted from "How we met: Arthur Williams & Rachael Latham – 'She says I'd make good husband material, but hopeless boyfriend material'" by Nick Duerden, *The Independent* 28.02.14. Copyright © The Independent; Adapted Text on p. 158 from Agenda, Summer 2013, News and Views from OCR/Summer 2013, www.ocr.org.uk. Reproduced by kind permission of OCR.

Photo acknowledgements

p. C1 (photo 5A): © Amanda Hall/robertharding/Corbis; p. C1 (photo 5B): © Mike Kemp/In Pictures/Corbis; p. C2 (photo 5C): Nicola Tree/The Image Bank/Getty Images; p. C2 (photo 5D): © Leonard Lenz/Corbis; p. C4 (photo 6A): Gallo Images – Robbert Koene/Gallo Images/Getty Images; p. C4 (photo 6B): © Andreas Pacek/Westend61/Corbis; p. C5 (photo 6C): © UpperCut Images/Alamy Stock Photo; p. C5 (photo 6D): © Andreas Pollok/Corbis; p. C7 (photo 7A): © Claudia Wiens/Corbis; p. C7 (photo 7B): © Thilo Brunner/Corbis; p. C8 (photo 7C): Eric Thayer/REUTERS; p. C8 (photo 7D): © Matthew Williams-Ellis/robertharding/Corbis; p. C10 (photo 8A): © Randy Lincks/All Canada Photos/Corbis; p. C10 (photo 8B): © Paul Thompson/Corbis; p. C11 (photo 8C): UniversalImagesGroup/Getty Images; p. C11 (photo 8D): © Chuck Savage/Corbis.

Visual materials for the Speaking test

What are the people enjoying about these guided tours?

5A

5B

Why have the people decided to exercise in these ways?

5C

5D

5E

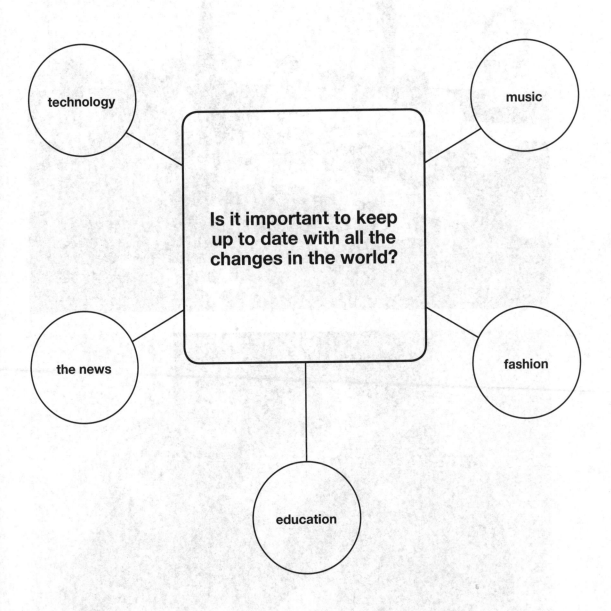

Why might it be important to give advice in these situations?

6A

6B

Art galery

Why are these people looking at these beautiful things?

6C

6D

On the roof.

6E

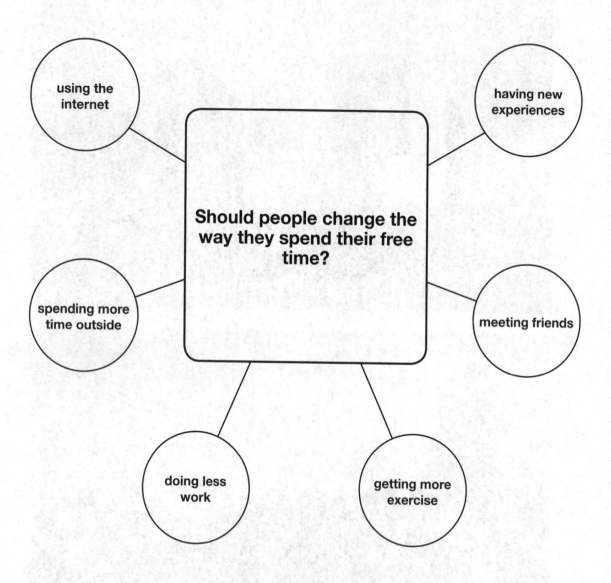

Why have the people decided to spend time in these quiet places?

7A

7B

On top of a mountain – a single man he is relaxing watch watching the view.

C7

fireworks

What might the people be enjoying about doing these things at night?

7C

7D

7E

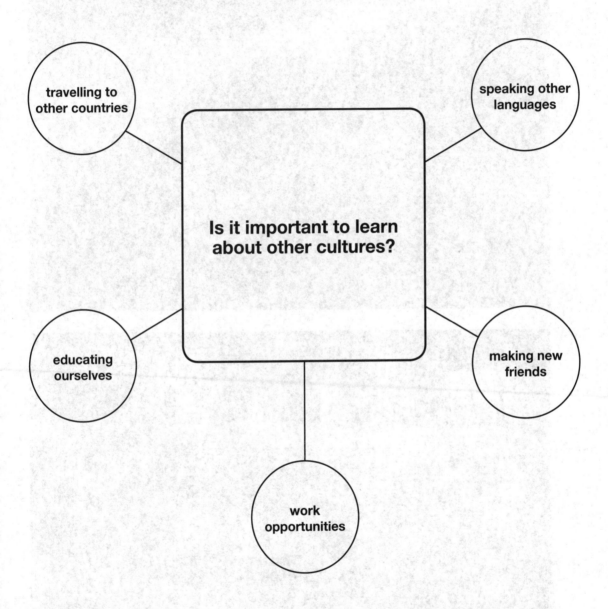

travelling to
other countries

speaking other
languages

Is it important to learn
about other cultures?

educating
ourselves

making new
friends

work
opportunities

Visual materials for the Speaking test

What are the people enjoying about spending time by the different rivers?

8A

8B

What are the people enjoying about being at these big events?

8C

8D

— concert (simphonic concert)

8E

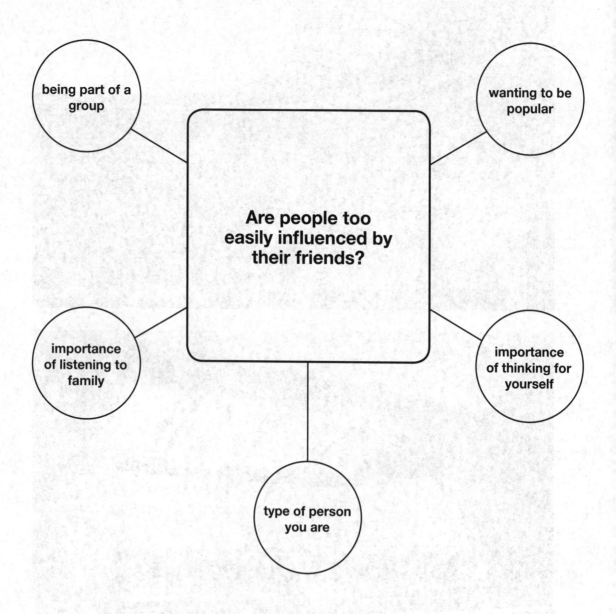

Cambridge English

OFFICIAL EXAM PREPARATION MATERIALS

CAMBRIDGE.ORG/EXAMS

What do we do?

Together, Cambridge University Press and Cambridge English Language Assessment bring you official preparation materials for Cambridge English exams and IELTS.

What does *official* mean?

Our authors are experts in the exams they write for. In addition, all of our exam preparation is officially validated by the teams who produce the real exams.

Why else are our materials special?

Vocabulary is always 'on-level' as defined by the English Profile resource. Our materials are based on research from the Cambridge Learner Corpus to help students avoid common mistakes that exam candidates make.

Authentic examination papers: what do we mean?

INVOLVING WRITING TEAMS AROUND THE WORLD

PRETESTING

VALIDATION

PRACTICE PAPERS

SELECTION

LIVE EXAMS

Testbank

NOW ALSO AVAILABLE ONLINE IN Testbank

Practice makes perfect!

Testbank

AUTHENTIC PRACTICE TESTS

FLEXIBLE APPROACH

IMPROVE CONFIDENCE

PERFECT PRACTICE

DETAILED GRADEBOOK

INSTANT MARKING

PROGRESS CHECKER

NOW ONLINE

TEST MODE

PRACTICE MODE

SPEAKING PRACTICE

Experience
'exam' conditions

Enhance learning
and practice

Timed video
simulation

Discover more
Official Preparation Materials

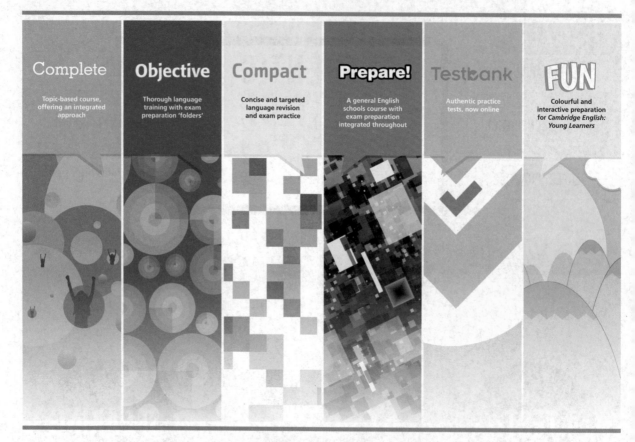

Courses, self-study,
learner support

CARDIFF AND VALE COLLEGE